CLAUDIA
WINKLEMAN

Quite

PRAISE (SORT OF) FOR *QUITE*

'A book? Hahahahaha'
Tilda, 14

'Seriously Mum, who's going to read this?'
Jake, 17

'Can I highly recommend a David Walliams instead?'
Arthur, 8

CLAUDIA WINKLEMAN

Quite

ONE PLACE. MANY STORIES

HQ
An imprint of HarperCollins*Publishers* Ltd
1 London Bridge Street
London SE1 9GF

This edition 2020

3

First published in Great Britain by
HQ, an imprint of HarperCollins*Publishers* Ltd 2020

HB ISBN: 978-0-00-842165-6
TPB ISBN: 978-0-00-842166-3
Exclusive edition HB: ISBN 978-0-00-842236-3
Special edition HB: ISBN 978-0-00-845150-9

Text design and typeset by Rosamund Saunders

Printed and bound in Great Britain by
CPI Group Ltd, Croydon CR0 4YY

MIX
Paper from
responsible sources
FSC
www.fsc.org FSC™ C007454

This book is produced from independently certified FSC™ paper
to ensure responsible forest management.

For more information visit: www.harpercollins.co.uk/green

For Jake, Tilda and Bear

CONTENTS

WELL,

_____

Quite

WELL,
HERE WE ARE

First things first, thank you so much for picking this up and considering a book from me – a short, orange woman who occasionally reads out loud on the telly. Even if you're going to chuck it to the other side of the bookshop, can I just say I'm extremely grateful. I am an enormous fan of a book, so am over the moon you are contemplating this one when we both know there are so many great ones on offer.

I want to be frank about what you can expect from me. If you're looking for a very serious tome, and you don't like anything flippant or trivial or lighthearted, or if you're interested in the Chartists or the pandemic or want to learn something practical and useful then this isn't the book for you.

Don't get me wrong, I have covered some pressing issues. I think I have been persuasive on the subject of voicemail and fairly brutal about the effect of fitting rooms on my wellbeing. I'm confident I have made a strong case for why you can't sleep with someone who doesn't have the vigour to get you both in a cab and I've had a good look at the reasons why spray tan and eyeliner are essential to my confidence.

I've tried to be as honest as I can, but it should be said that I am prone to exaggeration. At one point I say I'd be happy if the Christmas decorations went up in June but on reflection this probably isn't *quite* true. I love Christmas for many reasons but the amount of times I'd have to hoover pine needles from the living room floor over a six-month period doesn't bear thinking about.

I've written a little about art, because when I started to try to identify the things I really care about this came tumbling out, alongside quite a specific treatise about different sorts of boots. Great paintings have an enormous power to capture a moment, to really stop you in your tracks and make you completely forget about anything else, but we should all own boots that give off a certain attitude too. They have the power to make you walk like someone who is on their way to a wild party with a roguish rockstar, even if you are actually just going to Tesco Metro for some eggs.

I've also covered fringe maintenance, because my hair has basically given me a career. I talk about my kids a lot (they will never read this) and relationships (I've told my husband I've been freakishly positive about him – we're safe) and I fear I may have got a bit preachy when I write about good manners and wearing only black. I've also found that I have some quite strong opinions on the people we do – and definitely don't – need in our lives.

And why is it called *Quite*? Well, because it's my favourite word. It's a raised eyebrow, an aside. 'Well, *quite*.' But at the same time, it's firm, restrained and it manages your expectations:

'I think you'd quite like this film.'

'That egg sandwich was quite good.'

And that's what we need, I think. Things to be quite good. We're bombarded with a lot of images of 'perfect' these days – Instagram, fashion, general showing off. But perfect is boring. High expectations are a killer. It's certainly possible to make the perfect omelette (see page 193) and find the perfect t-shirt (takes work but is achievable, see page 132), but the perfect relationship? The perfect New Year's Eve? It's a solid no.

The thing about 'quite good' is that it leaves you somewhere to go. Because, so long as you have great friends, peanut butter and the opportunity for a nap then everything is broadly fine, and there is always the chance that something (or someone) will come along and blow your socks off. We all know that the best dates are the ones you almost didn't go on and the best nights out are those that were supposed to be just a quick vodka round the corner but ended up with dancing and laughing till the mascara ran down your face.

So I would like to make a case for the underrated and the imperfect. You can buy that very glamorous kaftan and you can spend three days planning the most impeccable dinner party, but you probably won't feel like Beyoncé on a yacht and the award-winning cheese board is not why the evening was fun. Can I recommend instead that you put on a good pair of jeans, smear (and I really do mean smear) some eyeliner in the vicinity of your eyelids and just go about your day. If the kids have done their homework, if the person you're with is kind and knows how to laugh at themselves, if you've remembered to call your best friend back then that is really quite good. Everything else is just sprinkles.

Quite
IMPORTANT
(TO ME)

NAPPING

Yes, on first glance this might feel like an odd place to start. Wait, I've just started reading, she's telling me to have a snooze? The answer is going to be an almighty yes. Yes to napping, yes to sleep, yes to being idle. I will explain …

When I was about twelve my mum had lunch with a brain surgeon. I'm not sure why. She was at a big work thing and, by happenstance, found herself sitting next to him. After an excellent and fascinating chat about how the brain works and funding for the NHS he said to her, 'By the way, always let your children sleep, it's the greatest life insurance we have. The brain grows and the body fixes itself while at rest. Anyway, have a great day, it was nice to meet you.' That's all he said, he didn't really elaborate and she didn't ask a gazillion questions but from that day onwards everything changed.

It wasn't subtle, it wasn't slow and there wasn't a big explanation. She came home and simply said, 'I will never tell you to get up at the weekends again.' I know, right? He must have been pretty compelling. And that was it. We were allowed, encouraged even, to get into bed. Homework's a bit tough? Stop looking at your physics and just get back under the covers and close your eyes. Here, I'll draw the curtains. Before we watch *Dynasty* why don't you curl up on the sofa and try and have a catnap? That's how it went.

It wasn't like that at my friends' houses. They were awed when I told them and most came back to mine on a Friday night and stayed till Sunday – four of us top to toe in a single bed. I had the only mother on earth who didn't come in at 9, 10 and 11am and say 'You're wasting the day.' She didn't sweep into my bedroom and open the curtains and announce, 'The weather is wonderful. Up you get, sleepyheads!' She'd let us sleep for hours. Midday would pass, even 1pm.

Lunch was moved later and later so my brother and I could laze about in our rooms. If either of us were still asleep then everyone had to be extra quiet so as not to wake us up. No radio, no TV, no loud chatting, absolutely no vacuuming or banging about with pots and pans. Shhh, she's asleep. She's growing and needs to rest. Why is the football so loud? I've told you, I think she might be catching 40 winks.

When people ask me about my childhood I remember all sorts of things. Screaming with laughter with my dad and sister, his pasta sauce, my step-mum's teriyaki steak on special occasions. I remember my mum getting ready and the clickety clack of high heels on pine floors and the smell of Giorgio Beverly Hills (we were so '80s) and watching *Trading Places* on a loop with my brother. But the main thing that comes to mind, my real resounding memory, is of napping.

Sleep was good for me; everyone was delighted when I slept. I woke up after a good ten hours only to pad downstairs, eat all the Sun-Pat I could find (I once had it on raw mushrooms, I don't advise) and then I'd trail back upstairs again, sometimes with a cup of tea or a Diet Coke and I'd get back into bed and manage maybe another 45 minutes.

I have not grown out of this – I still love napping now. In fact, I'm all for idleness, for doing nothing. I'm hugely in favour of taking a load off. I'm not sure when we equated 'busy' with success or doing nothing with wasting time. The implication is: you're so sluggish, so idle, so slovenly.

Can't talk now. Rush rush rush. I'm just so, so busy. Seriously, you thought I was hectic two months ago? That was nothing, I'm now so frantic I'm going to lose my head. We'll have to diarise a catch-up. Does next Thursday at 12.50 work? I'll have a free ten before lunch.

Most of us feel we're on hamster wheels – homework, cooking, showering, bedtime story, back downstairs, on our phones, watching the latest boxset (FFS put on *Tiger King*, we're days behind, I feel like an arsehole), meetings, weekend plans, calls, conference calls ('Hi, it's Phil here. I'm going to introduce six people on this call but then only I am going to talk. That's just me, cool') and then it's lunches and more meetings and racing home and changing and drinks and then out for supper and then home and too exhausted to brush teeth/have sex/laugh about Phil on the conference call and then it happens again. This may feel hard to avoid sometimes but I don't understand why it's to be lauded, why anyone thinks it's a *good idea*.

The really successful people – I mean the spectacularly smart ones – seem to be gardening and reading books and pottering about (have you seen their Insta stories? They're literally drinking martinis on a barge). Let's emulate that. Relax, don't show off about being busy, boast about being idle, then you've done something truly right.

And the best place to start in order to achieve this, I strongly believe, is napping. My bed is my safe place, my happy place and I don't think it should just be for nights. I'm happy to spring out of it at 7am and make three different breakfasts (you're right, my kids are totally spoilt, why don't they all like the same cereal?) and jump on the Central Line to drop the little one off. I whizz home with an enormous smile on my face because I know that, after a coffee and some radio, it's time to go back to sleep. My friends call it 'a meeting'. They'll text, 'Claud, call after your meeting.' When we're filming *Strictly*, I'll go in for the morning, rehearse, get two full spray tans (I simply can't present that show unless I've had a double dip) and then I'll just lie down on the sofa and get a quick 30 minutes.

I think I like napping because it feels slightly illegal, stolen, naughty. I'm not interested in actual rebellion (I used to hand in my homework early for god's sake) but a nap is about the right level for me. I can't advise enough that you should do it too. It's a small but lovely act of defiance of this mad rule that we should appear busy at all times.

To get you started, let me explain the basic nap laws that should be adhered to.

A MORNING NAP

This is for the beginner. You think you've slept enough? Don't be so sure. I am positive we can eke out a little more. This won't mess with your sleep in the night so it's a great one to start with. Your room shouldn't be pitch black but instead curtains half drawn and I recommend you do not submerge yourself under the duvet but instead choose a light covering. Use a blanket if you have one, or I often use the coat I've worn on the school run, or, in an emergency, a towel. Don't set an alarm as you'll naturally wake up after 30 or 45. A small warning: when you wake up you'll be ravenous. Please make sure there's bread and butter in the house.

A LUNCHTIME NAP

You must eat lunch *after* the nap. This is imperative as you'll fall into a better slumber if you're not too full. This can be done with blinds/curtains fully closed and phone on silent as it's such a special treat. A small note: you'll love this nap so much you'll cancel all future lunches. I know she's your best friend and she wants to meet in Pret for a tuna baguette and a catch-up but I'm afraid you'll want to chat on the phone at 3 instead.

If you're at the office sneak off into a cubicle or a pod (these things exist) and put on your headphones and turn away from everyone. They'll think you're 'working' and instead you'll shut down. Better than another talk about plans for the weekend and weak tea.

A LATE AFTERNOON NAP

I don't want to blow my own trumpet but this is only for the advanced napper and should not be attempted without prior experience. The truth is that this is pretty close to bedtime so it's quite risky. This is the bungee jump of naps, the parachute dive of sleeps.

It's 6pm and you're back from work. The kids are arguing, your husband wants to watch the latest Scandi thriller and you want some hula hoops and *Dirty Dancing*. You're stressed about dinner and all you have is a butternut squash (never good), some wholemeal pasta (please) and half a bottle of barbeque sauce (which is possibly off). There's only one thing for it – a nap. For this one you're going to need an alarm. Thirty minutes should do it but any more and we're in hazardous territory. Close the blinds and get under the duvet (I know). Shoes off but not pyjamas yet. You'll fall asleep incredibly fast and the buzz of the alarm will be annoying. Get up, brush teeth and come back into the kitchen a new woman ready to make squash soup and prepared to watch (another) dark murder mystery set in Oslo.

YOU MUSTN'T STAY WITH HIM IF …

Do you remember when she got together with him and we said it wouldn't last but they're still really happy together and it's *quite* weird but also lovely? Yes, exactly. Relationships are strange and what would be an absolute dealbreaker for one person is a sweet quirk to someone else. My husband and I fundamentally disagree about buffets and baby names yet we have made it work. That said, and I don't wish to be reductive here, but there are some lights-flashing, sirens-blaring, nailed-on warning signs that I strongly believe should never be ignored. Tell me if you disagree …

HE CAN'T GET A CAB

'Yeah, you're probably right, it's time to leave. I have a taxi app but I don't have much signal – do you know the wi-fi code here? Why don't we just see if we can find a taxi on the street? It's only a slight drizzle and your heels aren't *that* high. Or we could just wait and see if someone else is leaving this party soon and they could give us a lift if they're going in the same direction? Yes, let's just stand in the corridor here near the kitchen and see if anyone looks like they might be getting their coat.'

Um, come again? What? Pardon? Hello? Have you broken into another language? See you, dude. Night night. It's been fun flirting with you, I had thought you were cute, you made a joke about canoes and I believed this could be a thing. You're a bit wet though, a bit slow on the uptake. Please don't call me – in fact, delete me from your contacts. Will I be going back to yours so you can play with my knicker elastic for 30 minutes? I don't think so.

Look, I don't like a 'strong' man ('I could easily lift up this table. I'm really good at fighting, did that bloke look at you funny? Because I'll have him. Let me get that door for you babe – look, I almost took it off its hinges') but I do want someone to get me home or back to his with some urgency, with some speed, with a certain amount of vigour. It's raining – you stay here, I'll grab us a cab. Ring a ding ding. Hot, cool, assured, right there. Back to yours for a tequila on the rocks and an old Carrs cracker covered in Primula? Why not. I might even let you have a go on my boobs, the left one is award winning.

HE DOESN'T HAVE ANY FRIENDS

If you're fifteen and he hasn't found his tribe yet then sure, let him be a bit solo, a tiny bit lost. That's adorable, should be admired; take him under your wing and be his first kiss. Beyond this point, a man who hasn't collected people (I'm not talking about miniature ceramic collections here – any collectors of anything should generally be avoided) just isn't worth spending time on.

How has he got through life without knowing that the key is friendship, without having endless nights out laughing with mates? How can you even think about licking his neck if his contacts file is empty? Something's up, something's wrong. If he always wants to go out with *your* friends, to *your* parties, to sit on the sofa with *your* sister, this is all lovely, but where are his people? Where are his school friends, his work friends, his 'we met on a night bus and just clicked' friends? A man without a gang is not to be entertained. There's something off. Or he's married. Next.

HE SPLITS THE BILL

Look, I'm a staunch feminist, I'm all for equal everything and I don't need a man to keep me in shoes, cashews, under a roof, anything. But if he looks at the check on an early date and says, 'To be honest, the sparkling water is quite expensive here but I'm not going to make a thing about it – let's just go halves,' then you need to pick up the whole bill, leave a big tip and immediately exit from his life.

A generous man is what we're after. I want him to get the rounds in, to send his mum flowers on a random Thursday to cheer her up, I want him to book tickets to stuff, to buy you personalised Marmite just because he felt like it. I want whatever money he has to pour through his fingers. He might not have a mortgage or savings or a pension and his over-spending might be infuriating but it's still better than the other kind. (By the way, even if he does have a pension you don't want to hear about it. If a man ever starts a chat with, 'The funny thing is, I went with Scottish Widows,' then you must know he's going to bore you to tears within the first month. Also mate, define 'funny'.)

You know the ones – they keep a tally about who paid for what last in their friendship group, they frown every time you say you bought a new lipstick/scented candle/pen. He'll say, 'Sure, it's nice but did you need it?' I mean … What does *need* have to do with anything? These men weigh up the pros and cons of life by working out how much it will cost and this just isn't sexy.

I don't care if they have money or not, and of course it's absolutely fine for you to pay for everything, it's the constant halving I can't stomach and neither should you. Also, if he's not generous at the bar – 'Look at them, they just got engaged, let's send over a couple of glasses of wine' – then he's going to be absolutely useless in the sack. He'll be selfish, a bit too precise and he'll insist on a 'wipe down' afterwards (there's officially nothing worse). My girlfriends and I have tried and tested this fact so you don't have to.

HE BELIEVES IN STAR SIGNS

The second he looks at you (even if he's twinkly and witty and wearing great old jeans and an oversized fisherman's sweater) and says, 'I'm a Gemini so you could say I've got two sides,' you must pretend you left your Corby trouser press on and hurry home to sort it out immediately. Never look back, he's – I'm sorry but I can't be gentle about this – a moron. I'm not saying it's only OK to get naked with people with a PhD (although I'd highly recommend it) but if his knowledge of science has resulted in him believing a twelfth of the population behaves a certain way because they happen to be Capricorns you absolutely can't spend another moment with him, fisherman's sweater or not.

HE HAS AN OPINION ABOUT YOUR APPEARANCE

You're a little bit giddy about him, he has strong hands (you're right, that *is* code), he asks lovely questions about your brother and sister and you think he's funny. You've met his flatmate and he's charming and there's talk of a weekend away. How magnificent, is this *the one*? And then suddenly and seemingly out of nowhere, you start getting a little bit tense around him – you are extra conscious of making him happy.

The opinions started small – 'Wow, I really like it when you wear your hair up' – and then move onto, 'You should really wear tighter jeans, seriously, there's nothing wrong with looking sexy.' And all of a sudden it's, 'Why have you put on so much lipstick? You know I prefer it when you wear just a light gloss, why don't you nip to the bathroom to wipe it off so we can enjoy our night?'

Please understand that none of this is about what you look like; it's about making you feel slightly small, slightly nervous, just a bit less than – it's about control. If he's nuts about you (and of course he should be) he won't really care or notice if you're in a tracksuit, a ball gown or wearing a full squirrel fancy dress costume (OK, he probably will notice that one) but he'll love you for everything that you are. You can be a goth, in baggy clothes, just back from a run, in the tightest top on the planet. It's all gravy, it's all fine. Do not try to please him with your appearance, just like you wouldn't expect him to change his for you. Unless of course he wears top-to-toe Hackett in which case you have my permission to 'accidentally' put all his striped polo tops on a boil wash. That's just sensible.

HE GIVES YOU ANYTHING WITH A PLUG

I don't need bouquets and I don't need jewellery. I'm not turned on by a teddy bear holding a squidgy heart with my name on it. I actually don't need presents. My husband once bought me a large piece of mature cheddar and a bottle of Lea & Perrins and it was possibly the greatest gift I've ever received. Men don't have to spend cash to be extra special. But I don't want (definitely in the early days) an appliance. It gives the wrong message, it's deeply functional and it doesn't make me want to wrap my legs round him. My friend is still going out with a man who gave her a bread maker and she's still angry about it. He's funny and kind and sweet and they got through it but she did have to explain she wasn't his cook, his mum. We know it's a great iron, the best hair dryer in the world, a fantastic deep fat fryer. You want one for the flat? Sure, makes sense. Please don't dress it up in Santa Claus wrapping paper and say you think it's what I've always wanted. It isn't.

HE OWNS (AND USES) EYE CREAM

Men have to walk a fine line here and I don't envy them. Do I want to get into bed with him if he's got dirt under his fingernails and his groin smells like an unwashed camel? Not particularly. But I'd still prefer to spend a weekend with that guy rather than the man who spends fifteen minutes in front of the mirror every morning applying a variety of face creams. Vanity isn't great for women, it's actually unattractive in all humans, but it's utterly appalling for a man you're considering having a relationship with.

'Sorry babe, can you step aside a second, I just need to see my reflection. Very happy for you to stay the night, but there are a few house rules, this here is my toner which I bought in duty free. I'd like you to leave it alone if possible as it's particularly good for my skin type. I've noticed a real difference. Here, have a feel.' Um … Of course you want him to be clean, but at the same time completely uninterested in his appearance. 'Feel my arms, I worked out for an hour today' is a bigger passion killer than 'come back to mine, I've got three tarantulas in a glass cage, I let them roam free round the bedroom while I'm sleeping and they like hiding in my hair.'

HE SAYS HE'LL BABYSIT HIS OWN CHILDREN

Well, you can't just up and leave, I realise it's a bigger decision than that. You're together, you decided to procreate with him. But the second he says it, and I do mean the *second*, you have to put him straight. 'Don't worry, you go out with the girls and I'll babysit the kids.' Dude, they're *yours*. You're simply not babysitting. I've seen this countless times – it's amusing maybe once, it's completely infuriating twice.

IF HE TALKS ABOUT HIS CAREER BUT YOUR JOB

This is subtle. It's small. I'm not saying it's the death knell but it's certainly giving you a little clue. You're only six months in and he's up for a promotion. I get he might be nervous and it's cute to make him a lucky packed lunch. But the tiny difference in language here might grow if you don't gently tread on it. You both either have jobs or you both have careers. End of.

HE'S THE BEST LOOKING MAN IN THE ROOM

This is ridiculous I know. You are no doubt laughing at me now. But hear me out. I've met extremely attractive men, I've interviewed tons of off-the-scale-knockout males. Should I sit here, Brad? Why did you choose this particular script, George? Of course I can get you a glass of water, Harrison. Lovely little eight-minute moments all of them, but would I want to go out with any of them? Definitely not.

Very handsome men have always had to make – and this is a shame – very little effort. They turn up and smile and that's it. They can yawn at dinner, they can pick their nose while driving the car. They can only talk about themselves and not ask a question and they can get up and leave early or arrive late. Very good-looking men are nice to have about, great to be friends with, but don't make them your life partner. Their lack of wit, energy and effort will drive you mad after the lust and 'check out who I'm shagging' has gone.

SWAGGER

Look, this is a chapter about boots.

But I need to say from the off, it's not *actually* about footwear.

Boots are not just something you put on your feet. When you shop for them, they're not a 'these will do, add to basket' and when they're part of your outfit, they're not a small addition, an afterthought.

They are the whole look. The reason you're out. The reason he looked at you funny. The reason you feel like a rockstar, walking backstage at the O2.

I know what you're thinking – 'She's gone and lost it now. Maybe it's the fumes from the fake tan.' Sure, that's completely possible. But let me expand.

Boots are, above all, about attitude. They are not simply objects that stop your feet getting dirty. Of course there's your hair and your heavy armload of bangles that turn your wrists green (correct, totally worth it) and your big sack of a bag (the same one you've had since the 90s, something totally cool about that) but your real calling card, your actual, well, assertiveness comes from your feet.

If you can walk into a bar with a look that says 'I can use ornery in a sentence but I also just might have a trick pelvis' then that's coming from your boots. They are the reason you can turn up slightly late for a lecture at university and give the impression you've just done it with your boyfriend behind the bins, just got shortlisted for a literary prize, just listened to the latest Rolling Stones track because you're an old friend of Keith's. These things won't be true but you might want it to seem that they are. And this will not be achieved through your choice of pencil case, or because you're wearing a lip stain or a nose stud. This, my friends, is radiating from your feet.

You are walking to meet a date at the cinema for the first time. You want to waltz up to the kiosk (don't actually waltz, unless of course you're seeing *La La Land*) with all the must-iness of Debbie Harry or Nick Cave. That's not just in your fingerless gloves (although I do applaud) and it's not in your hoop earrings. Apart from your sparkly eyes, or slight air of disdain, the thing that will stay with him is your all-round vibe and that is emanating from below your knees.

I knew boots were special when I walked past Shelley's when I was fourteen and saw some pointy, aggressive, spiky ones in the window. 'Can we go in Dad, please can we go in?' I begged.

'Don't be mad baby, it's getting late and we still need to get peppercorns' (people were obsessed with these in 1986).

They were ankle-high with a livid, thin heel. Even then, staring though the window (in my flat, black, round-toed shoes from Dolcis – please) I knew they could change my life. 'There you are my babies,' I thought to myself. 'You're going to make me feel wholly different.' They were so grown up, so rebellious, so unbelievably cool. I had never seen such a thing. They were a passport to a different world.

Here's the thing, you do not need to buy new jeans un-less they become literally unwearable – I wear the same ones I bought fifteen years ago (yes, I can't do up the button); t-shirts and sweaters generally look better if they're old, beaten, torn and slightly mothy. Coats keep the cold out and, although they have to be fantastic (nothing collarless please), you'll take it off when you get to the party/pub/dinner. You can say absolutely all you need to say with a pair of boots. They instil a power, a fuck-off attitude, a certain defiance. If you pick right (I have gone into some detail on page 26) then they alone will give you all the confidence you need.

Have you seen *Desperately Seeking Susan*? Well, she trades in her magical and lucky leather jacket for a pair of sparkly stiletto bunched-up boots. Exactly that. That's what we're after, that's what every woman needs.

I had a bad row with my mum over a pair of boots. I was sixteen. We were away on holiday in Spain and it was unbelievably hot. It was boiling, seriously sweltering, and we were going down to the hotel restaurant for dinner. My brother is eight years younger than me so this was unusual; because he was little we'd normally just get chips in our room and he'd be put to bed early and I'd read (often in the bathroom so as not to wake him up) and then I'd turn out the lights when I was tired. But this night was different, it was fancy, an occasion, something to remember. We'd talked about it all day; he'd had a nap in preparation for staying up late and I was excited about trying something called calamari that everyone was talking about.

It was a fisherman's catch buffet night and I was a little bit in love with a boy who was there with his family. I'd stared at him solidly for six days straight at the pool. I'd laughed too loudly at breakfast so he looked round. We once bumped heads in the entrance hall when I was walking in and he was walking out (in my mind we were getting married) so I laid out my outfit extremely carefully. Over the miniature thimble of grapefruit or tomato juice we were going to lock eyes and that would be it, my first full-on boyfriend (I was, uh, a slow developer).

Did I mention it was hot? Like 100 degrees. I wanted to wear my black sundress and my (wait for it) knee-high, fake suede, platform, studded boots. They were from C&A and they were pure magic. It was my plan, it was part of the story. He'd see me in them, he'd realise that I was fashionable, nonchalant, on trend and practically an adult. I backcombed my hair, I put on some lip-liner (yes, it was chocolate brown, boof) and I was ready to go.

But my mum, who was always pretty casual on clothes and what I wanted to wear (she never needed us to look 'just so', she didn't have the time), said no. She explained it was scorching; I'd look nuts and I should wear flip flops like everyone else. I tried to plead, I begged, I said it was important but she just refused. You're not going downstairs, in this heat, in those clunky, sweaty boots. Don't be ridiculous.

I nodded sulkily and we went down for a prawn surprise and other glamorous things but I couldn't shake it off. I didn't speak and grew more and more upset. I just sat silently looking down at my hands. Normally I was bouncy, usually I'd make everything nice and generally I always behaved.

After twenty minutes hot steam began to pour from my mother's ears. 'What is it? Why are you ruining supper? Why aren't you talking?'

'I wanted to wear my boots,' I said quietly.

'Fine, go get them and then please come down here with a smile.'

I went to my room and changed my shoes. Sure, I looked weird. Yes, I was melting and truthfully the faux suede never really recovered. But did I have a great night? Absolutely. We ate fresh fish, I stared at the boy I liked, my family ended up playing Uno while eating lemon ice cream that was served in actual lemons and I went to bed happy. Was it about the boots? Was it about the boy? Not really. It was about something much more important – it was about confidence. Even then, as a spotty, heavy fringed, patchy tanned, glasses-wearing teenager, I knew that in those boots I had swagger.

And swagger is what every girl and woman deserves. Everything else is hard enough. We're on the hamster wheel of life. Yes, she's got her PE kit, yup, bridge is on for 8pm and what's that? You've both given up meat, dairy and anything raw? No problem, I'll rustle up some, um, warm nuts. Our boss wants another meeting about when to have another meeting and our parents have said they'd like us to go away with them on a camper van holiday for the bank holiday. The traffic is gridlocked, the papers are full of bad news, the bank has decided that our overdraft has gone on for too long and the kids have seen a mouse in the kitchen. We rush and we negotiate and we hustle to keep everything on track – which is all made just a bit easier if we are doing it whilst wearing a pair of truly great boots.

Perhaps you already own these boots and you have been nodding along in agreement. If you have yet to meet your most empowering, enabling footwear, please use this list to help you identify the boots that are right for you.

THE LEGAL SECRETARY

This is a heavy, blocked heel option with a no-nonsense attitude. Wear with black crepe trousers for work and with an oversized polo neck and jeans at the weekend. An aside: if boots can be worn every single day then that's better. Don't save boots 'for best' – there is no best.

THE GROUPIE

You want to feel like you might be going back to the drummer's place for a heavy goblet of vodka and some filth? Where the music will be on really loud and people are getting up to mischief on the pool table? No, of course we're not actually going to do that (it sounds like a lot of effort and way too messy), but these high-heeled ankle sex boots will make you feel like the option is available.

THE NEW MUM

You can't shift the baby weight. You're boring yourself rigid about why she likes broccoli but not carrots and the school run is genuinely killing you – I've just dropped her off, how can I be going back again so soon? You haven't been on a night out in months and while you're having sex with your husband you're doing the weekly shop in your head. These are not ballet flats (never fine, unless you're actually doing ballet) and they're not slippers (guys …). They are still great boots but they do not involve laces (designers, if we had time to do our laces as well as everyone else's we'd let you know), you do not have to sit down to put them on and they can be thrown by the front door. Excellent with jeans and a massive shirt (that you might have slept in).

THE INTELLECTUAL

These are akin to a classic brogue but slightly more interesting than a Chelsea boot. They're best in tobacco or cinnamon (real boot colours) and look much better when worn for years. Buy and then give them to a friend's dog to gnaw at. Leave them out in the garden so they get a bit soiled and wear them hard. Day in, day out. Wear them if you're walking in some fields (it might actually be worth a visit to the countryside) and, when they're broken in, then they will come to the fore. Brilliant when paired with a battered satchel and overly long scarf.

STYLES TO BE AVOIDED

- The fringed moccasin boot (only OK on Kate Moss and Pocahontas, absolutely not fine for anyone else)

- The almond toe (too indecisive: either a square or a point, what is this?)

- The over-the-knee (cheap, even though unbelievably expensive)

- The boot with a logo (we get it, you've got money. Pipe down)

- The kitten heel (if you want your calves to look like massive hams then go ahead but otherwise it's a solid no)

- The sock boot (make it stop)

- The cowboy (fine if you're in a rodeo and even then …)

- The Ugg (look, I know they're comfy but so are onesies and adult nappies)

A SMALL
LECTURE
ABOUT ART

We were sixteen, we were deeply pleased with ourselves, extraordinarily annoying and thought we already knew everything. We'd all picked history of art because we thought it would be a doddle. Yes Miss, we know about paintings. Yes Sir, we get that sculpture might be made of marble. Duh. Yes, we can spell Michaelangelo (wait a second, is that right?) and of course we go to galleries (do they serve cider there and are they full of cute boys?).

For context – I went to an all-girls school bang in the centre of London, we flew to school on the tube, had a full burgundy uniform (even tights #speechless). We were a hotchpotch of badly executed home-highlights, Juicy Fruit gum and an unhealthy obsession with whether to go to third base.

Our skirts were rolled up too high, two of us wore fishnets (burgundy ones, yes, they exist), we passed notes to each other and we stared out of the window dreaming that Simon le Bon would waltz in and save us. Can you imagine anything worse than teaching us? Exactly. Me neither.

Our history of art teacher was Mrs Dale. She was pristine,

she was calm, she was together. She wore a high bun and at least eight different shades of brown. She hardly raised her voice, she never yelled, she rarely tutted. She was kind, she was quiet, she had pin-sharp focus and she believed in loafers and the Renaissance.

One morning, we were (as usual) not paying attention, almost certainly whispering about lunch – I'll swap a Marathon bar for a bagel, sure – and she said, 'Right class, nothing seems to be going in while we're here. Let's go and see something, shall we?' She shot up from behind her desk faster than a whippet on crack and marched out of the classroom at high speed. Confused and still talking about the merits of a Double Decker versus a Flake, we all got up to follow her.

She sprinted to the school's front door and we practically had to run to keep up. 'What's the matter with her?' we mouthed as our teeth clattered together – it was a freezing January day and there was no time to get our coats. It was windy, we were swearing under our breath, she was striding with purpose. She trooped us to St Paul's Cathedral. We didn't understand, we asked if this was a planned trip, we occasionally called out, 'You alright, Miss?' but we followed her in and were immediately hushed. The chatting stopped.

'Now, girls. I know lunch is important, I know boys are irresistible, but you need to understand what we're studying here. Breathtaking architecture, mesmerising art, wonderful sculpture. *That* is the greatest privilege of all.' Her hands were on her hips (this meant business we'd later learn).

She continued. 'I was young once, I understand you just want to gossip and natter and have fun, but look up. Don't worry about lipstick and bands and anything else at this moment. I implore you, girls. Just. Look. Up.'

We'd walked past the cathedral a million times, we'd sat on her steps while scoffing Monster Munch ogling boys from the school opposite, we'd taken her for granted. The inside of St Paul's is (and I really do hate this word but it's the only one that will do) awesome. It's enormous, it's majestic, it's classical architecture in its purest form and the dome is 365 feet high. The columns feel like they reach space, the nave could house fifteen buses (this is not strictly true but it feels like it) and it took our breath away.

Mrs Dale encouraged us to take it all in while she explained Lord Admiral Nelson and Sir Christopher Wren were buried there. She let us gawp at the detailing while telling us that Martin Luther King chose St Paul's to give a sermon in 1964. 'It only just survived the blitz, it's a masterpiece, don't forget this. The whole design came from one brain. This is on our doorstep, art is alive and if I need to distract you from tittle tattle to wake you up, then so be it.'

Of course we didn't want to look like we'd turned, we didn't want to look too impressed. But something happened that day. There was nothing funny to hide behind. We couldn't take the mick, we couldn't whisper and laugh. It was just us, looking at Wren's masterwork. We stayed too long, we missed lunch and we were in the palm of her hand from that day forward. She talked to us like we were grown-ups, she fed us with information without thinking it wouldn't go in. She didn't panic about note-taking and underlining essay titles. She didn't sweat the small stuff.

Not long after our spontaneous trip to St Paul's, Mrs Dale casually took us to the National Gallery to stand in front of the *Arnolfini Portrait* for 90 minutes one day after school. Then, the following year, she successfully fought with the headmistress for money to take us to Italy. 'They *need* to see it,' she was heard yelling just outside the lunch hall. It was 1989 and we were seventeen and we went to Venice. The whole history of art A level group – about twelve of us. It was bats.

Some of us had been away with our families but it was usually beach holidays or camping – we were about to experience something else entirely. When the plane landed and we got into a boat (wow, they weren't kidding, there really is a lot of water,

I thought it was, like, one river) we were blown away. We were there for two nights and three full days. We'd never seen anything like it, a whole city, like, on water (we said 'like', like, *all* the time).

We went to the Accademia and gazed up at the Raphaels. We ate all the gelato we could find and barely slept, staring out of the window gazing at the church spires and little gondolas. We ate pasta in tiny backstreets. 'Look at that little bridge over the canal, look, they live there, in that apartment, the one that you get to by boat. Can you imagine?' we squealed. This was a whole other world, this was a living, breathing, artwork that doubled up as an actual city. We wafted round St Mark's Square feeling romantic and grown up and were just completely wowed. We shared an £8 coffee (so adult) and flirted with any poor unsuspecting boy we could find. *Ciao! T'Amo!* I mean, Venice should have ejected us.

Mrs Dale must have loved seeing our faces and gaping mouths. 'Come on girls, here's the Rialto, keep up, I'm now going to show you a Gorgione that might make you realise the power of storytelling through painting. And wait till I tell you what an x-ray of this painting revealed. Come on, come on.'

On the last day, we were all crowded round a table tearing through pizza and she said, quite indifferently, 'You have 30 minutes of free time now and then I'd like you to meet me at the back of the Basilica Maria Gloriosa dei Frari. We'll stay there for a bit and then collect our bags and go to the airport.' So we spent the next half hour mooching around the tiny shops looking at elaborate masks and small animals made of glass – can anyone lend me some lira? I think I'll get my brother this tiny penguin – and then we slowly wended our way to the Frari.

It's not a beautiful church. It's large and hefty and absolutely fine but compared to some others in Venice (see San Giorgio Maggiore or Santa Maria Formosa) it is, at best, a B. It's large and red brick and although built in the sixteenth century could also be new. We slunk through the main doors at the end of the nave wondering where our teacher was and talking about if we had enough money to buy chocolate at the airport. The church was dark, it was enormous and a bit cold. Someone remembered she said to meet us at the back. Come on gang, last one. Bagsy have the Walkman on the plane first. God that pizza was good. I wish they had a heater in here. Now, where is Mrs D? We were done, we were sleepy, we were already back to life as normal and we just thought we'd get this out of the way and then get home. And then something happened. To be specific, Titian happened.

The *Assumption of the Virgin* is huge – it's 22 feet tall and it towers over you; the figures are larger than life-size, in every way. The Virgin Mary is being propelled up to god in heaven. I am not religious but I would believe in anything looking at her. It's a whirlwind, a painting that doesn't stand still. As with all of Titian's work it's the colour that winds you, that makes your legs give way. The red, the blue, the golden light – it is not of this world, it is not what we usually see, it is not mortal. We couldn't imagine this was real.

You see, you can't believe it's been created by human hand. The Virgin Mary looks like she's alive, her clothes hang like velvet, she's looking up, god is waiting for her. Beneath her, St Peter and the apostles are moving, they're alive, they're agitated, they're angst-ridden, they can't believe what they're seeing and this broke with all tradition. It's also in its rightful home: Titian painted it for this very church and this very spot (so often we see altarpieces in galleries, not in their 'natural habitat'). There is such emotional power, such energy, such life, such force.

There was a low level hum of wonder around that painting. We stood with other visitors in complete silence, absolutely agog with astonishment. We had never seen anything like it and to this day it remains the most extraordinary 'art moment' of my life (I'm lucky, I've had a few). We were struck – make that thunderstruck – by what one could arguably say is the greatest painting in the world. We stood there actually unable to speak. I don't know how many gaggles of seventeen-year-old girls you've come across but this is almost a miracle, an impossibility. We were quiet, we were thoughtful and didn't want to leave that particular painting. We were dumbstruck all the way home – nobody worried about sweets or looking at the other school trip on our plane rammed with boys.

When we got back to school we had to write about Titian's piece and we all said it was the greatest thing we'd ever seen. You see, every other altarpiece that came before it was polite, was proper, they followed the rules. There was beauty, yes, but that kind of energy? Absolutely not. This was a stand-out piece, something we knew we'd talk about in years to come. We asked Mrs Dale why she hadn't told us what we were about to see, why she'd just said to meet at the back of the church. She raised an eyebrow. 'Girls,' she said, 'you'll learn that, in life, high expectations are a killer.'

Of course, she is completely right and I have never forgotten that truth. Don't expect to have your mind blown, your feet swept up from under you. Don't think that you're going to have the best night, the best sex, the best job, the best life. Good to keep your hopes small, excellent to keep them low. Go see a film before you've read too many five star reviews, try that local Italian place before everyone on your street tells you the risotto is to die for. Avoid the hype and, equally, try not to oversell everything before people get a chance to see it for themselves.

I love being all knowing – you must watch this, you must read this, this will knock your socks off – but it's cruel in a way. Let people discover alone, let them have their own eureka moment. Send them the book, drop the name of the film or mention the band – don't tell them it will change their life as then it might not. Mrs Dale made art relevant, exciting, magical and most of us fell in love with it and continued to study/ read about it/talk about it to this day. (I'm writing about it now and this happened 100 years ago.) When I wanted to go to university I couldn't imagine learning about anything else. I loved literature, I loved classics but it had to be art. I specialised in Rembrandt and I still bore my kids rigid with stories about seventeenth-century Holland. Is it useful for *Strictly*? No. Is it useful for my soul? Totally.

You see, I don't know much, but I do know that art is the answer. Of course, there's eye shadow, great necking and heavy black coats, but looking up at a beautiful painting is about the most enriching thing you can do with your time. People talk about self-care and they'll talk animatedly over a hummus sandwich about bath salts and meditation and yoga. That's all well and good but popping into any place where there are paintings or sculptures dotted around is like an internal massage; it's better than humming on a mat and at it's very best – and this is big – it's even better for your soul than mascara.

The next time you feel slightly wobbly, the next time you feel confused, go to a gallery. Go to any. If you're in London spend half an hour in the National. It's free, it's next to a tube and its walls are genuinely the best in the world. You might love Van Eyck, you might be a Titian girl like me or you might just fall in love with Stubb's horse. Whatever you like, the colours, the sweeping brush strokes, the majesty will carry you up into a different world.

We accept mediocrity all the time. The pasta is edible, the music on the radio is passable, the bus was a bit late but at least there was a seat. We get the kids to bed, we check their spellings, we make sure our friends are fine and we pour ourselves a glass of wine at 8 and then flop into bed after the news. We get by. Of course we're grateful and we love our lives, but we're not always aware of extraordinary feats. Just sometimes we need to be reminded of gobsmacking, heart-thumping, stop-you-in-your-tracks beauty.

I realise that, at this point, you might be saying to yourself 'That short, orange lady off the telly is lecturing me about going to galleries' and considering throwing this book into the recycling bin. 'I bought this book for stories about Anton du Beke for god's sake,' you'll mutter into your coffee. 'I need the info on the *Strictly* curse, I absolutely refuse to hear about how Turner can change your life.'

But honestly, trust me in this one, and at least consider giving it a go. Don't worry about a calming app, don't spend a fortune on a life-enhancing eye cream (it won't) and don't worry about missing out on the latest boxset. Surround yourself with stunning works, just stop and look at one piece, give yourself twenty minutes to marvel in splendour and then go about your day. These artists have given us extraordinary gifts and it's a mistake to ignore them. Go and be amazed.

If you can get to Venice I'd like to meet you there – first Saturday in February at 2pm? Though I realise I've built her up now, I realise I've done everything Mrs Dale said I shouldn't. You won't be wowed so please let's forget what I said. Let's say it's just some oils on some wood, let's pretend it's something some bloke painted in 1515, some guy who was particularly good with the colour red. Am sure you've seen better, it's not a big deal. Meet you at the back of the Frari (I'll bring the tissues).

HERE COMES THE SUMMER

I'm going to come straight out with it. I don't believe in summer. It's all toes out (not fine) and enormous bottles of water and shoestring strap dresses and finding a tiny bit of earth to lie down on. It's a heightened, terrifying collective joy and a rushing panic that plans need to be made.

In October, when people ask, 'What are you doing at the weekend?' it's casual, it's easy breezy. You reply, 'Pub, maybe a book, that new Netflix show, we might finish the salami,' and it's put to bed. There's some relaxed nodding and everyone moves on.

But when May, June rolls around and there's a shard of light through the clouds and the weather app promises warmth, suddenly the questions are insistent, pointed and anxious in tone. Are you going to the park? Which one? Having friends round? I'm thinking of giving Jamie's haloumi wrap a go. What drinks will you make? Got a blender for the daiquiris? Want to borrow mine?

There's a strange zeal in the air, too much anxiety placed on just an afternoon. Two months ago and the whole weekend could be summed up by 'a puzzle, some soup, afternoon sex', but now you have to go into great detail. You pretend you have a garden (I do this) and mention re-potting a plant and doing something with weeds.

When friends come round in November a takeaway is fine; July arrives and suddenly you need to look for wooden bowls and matching salad servers (who has these?) and everyone is keen on ironed table linen and Pimms (any drink that needs cucumber to perk it up should be ashamed of itself).

Summer clothes are appalling – too much skin, too floral, too jaunty, too colourful. They're all well and good in rural Italy when your skin is olive and your boyfriend has an old, clapped-out convertible Fiat and your grandma has some sort of ancient trestle table that's always groaning under fresh lemons (with actual leaves attached) and mammoth jugs of wine. Then it makes sense. Sure, get your feet out, wear a sunshine yellow flowery midi dress, play summer music and stick on some body shimmer. But if you live in the UK then summer just won't do. It should be illegal.

Basically, it should be full-time Winter here. Yes, I used a capital letter on purpose. Winter is twinkly lights and capes and roasted chestnuts and gravy and stews. Winter is skinny black jeans and dishevelled boots and chaotic hair and sex panda eye make-up. It is not shimmery gloss and flip flops. Winter is let's huddle up at home at 4pm because it's dark outside and why not, I'll make mash and pour me a Baileys, babe.

Summer is too much pressure, too much high pitched squeals, too much forced fun. It's blockbusters that are too loud and too long and music festivals rammed with people off their heads eating candy floss and wearing 'I'm mad, me' hats.

In summer mistakes can't be made because the light is too bright, it's too honest, nothing can be hidden under wool and denim. The fake tan has to be flawless, the bra needs to not be too tight and the cuticles need to be clean – all that endless sunlight shows up the errors. Parties start with good intentions and aggressively marinated meats at 3pm and drag on forever as it never gets dark. People are hammered and messy at 9, they're slurring their words and falling off chairs and it's still basically supermarket lighting outside.

Hideous food is passed round (beetroot and feta tarts; lettuce and fennel wraps) and upbeat music is played (I loathe upbeat music, I like sullen, grumpy tunes). There's a frittata (can we just call it an omelette please?) and there's hysteria about the barbecue. We all have to stand round and watch a man with a pair of tongs feeling like Tarzan. Wow, he turned the sausages, you've got a good one there! He torches (sorry, cooks) the food and then we all have to nod and agree that the addition of turmeric in chipolatas really is the best thing ever.

Grown-ups feel young in the heat. In the winter we know our place, we behave like old people, we act our age – it's all crosswords, maybe some crochet or a brainteaser, we go to book clubs and eat toasties and get under our heavy duvets at 10pm. In summer, everyone goes barmy because they feel like teenagers. Adults walk around in baseball caps and 50-year-olds buy Converse hi-tops. Women who are usually happy in cardigans photograph themselves in hot pants, bunches and sucking ice lollies. Men stop wearing socks and organise frisbee in the park and the kids are up till midnight because their parents have got the karaoke out and the neighbours are round for prosecco and plates of parma ham with melon.

Summer then, please wake me when it's over.

A FRINGE

I'm not going to tell you to get a fringe like me. I'm not going to tell you to dye your hair dark brown like mine. And I'm not going to say the answer to life is hair falling in your face 24/7. In fact, if you're prone to conjunctivitis it could be a terrifically bad idea. You might loathe my fringe (I have a lot of letters to prove it's not, um, to everyone's taste) but, and I'm being perfectly serious here, it's given me a career.

I'm sure I got work because all those times producers were in a room ruminating on the next TV show, handing round digestives and they couldn't remember names, they said, 'We could always get the orange one with the fringe.' Believe me, it's not because I read out loud better than anybody else, it's not because I hold a microphone with an extra special grip, it's not because I can ask someone their name and where they've come from with more class. It's because I have a thing, an epithet, a focus (OK, I don't always have focus, mainly just a haircut, but you get the idea). Finding a uniform, a look, is simply a good plan.

When we were young, we liked playing around with what we wore. Ooh, it's sunny today I'm going to be a double-denim girl and maybe I'll tie that old gingham shirt with a knot so it's a jaunty crop top. To complete the ensemble, I'm going to need peach blush and I might just draw on some freckles.

Then, a month later, you'd give grunge a good go for its money – I've worn this t-shirt to bed for four days and these jeans are covered in crumbs and gin, so I'll do my eye make-up and then wipe it off with the back of my hand, leaving just a blue/black tinge. I'm so emo. I look like a thinker, actually maybe I'll carry around that Turgenev I'm never going to read too.

Some weeks later, you'd see a friend at a party in a layered tulle skirt and leather jacket and become convinced that Cyndi Lauper had it right all along – until, that is, your head is turned by an ad featuring a woman walking purposefully on a New York City street. You'd immediately think, hold on, what I *actually* need to do is embrace trench coats, poker straight hair and an enormous bag.

We all did it and it's important. We were trying people on, working out which felt the best.

Many of us carry on doing this right through university and even when we start work. Look at Alice, everyone respects Alice; I think it's because she's wearing Adidas Gazelles in dark grey. If I get Adidas gazelles I'll belong and Alice will like me and then I'll definitely do really well in this job . Oh, look at that, she's added some stick-on black sequins onto her lanyard – I should do that too. Best to fit in, best to be like Alice.

And then, one day, quite out of nowhere, we're frankly just too bloody knackered, too worn-out and no longer interested in the dressing up of it all. Am I going to go full siren in a pencil skirt today or should I go for masculine tailoring and a red lip? Am I thinking Sharon Stone here or should I go a bit Mel B? That leopard blazer is good, but too much with the handkerchief hem skirt from ASOS … We yawn, mutter how getting dressed can be hard work and it's then we realise that it's time to take it easy, take a load off, put our feet up and just decide.

Of all the people we were trying on, one will feel a bit easier, a little more comfortable, a little bit more like you. Your look might be 'the girl with all the bangles' or the 'woman who only wears bottle green' (this would actually be excellent) or you might be the human who can't live without extremely baggy personalised dungarees. Of course, it might be more subtle – it might be that you always have streaky hair, you might always revert to bronzer. Whatever your thing is, embrace it, own it, invest in it and keep it. It's now your adjective, your moniker, your handle if you will.

Mornings are no longer stressful. All the tulle/gingham/too-ripped jeans/black goth capes need to be chucked in a bag and taken to the charity shop. At this point in your life, seriously consider using a smaller cupboard. Into this compact space go the trousers you like, the tops you like, a pair of boots and maybe a couple of coats. Now you know what 'you' looks like, the clothes all match, they can be thrown on in any combination without thinking. That's it. I know that magazines talk about a hideous-sounding 'capsule wardrobe' (we're not going to the moon, FFS) but in this instance they are actually bang on. Choose a colour, choose a haircut (I also chose a tan shade – on the Dulux chart it's called 'terracotta: dark') and commit.

You will save time, you will feel comfortable shopping knowing that only one thing will do. I went through so many phases (the one that sticks out was the electric blue bow tie worn with a man's shirt and trousers entirely made of tapestry and no, you can't see a photo) and it was so relaxing to finally opt for pirate meets French male mature student in November. It was just the easiest look. I like dark, I like messy, I like pointy shoes. Hello, this will be me. Done.

If it's black or navy then it's a yes, if it's narrow jeans then it's a yes, if it's a big sweater then boom and if it's a pea coat and roughed up footwear then we're winning. Sure, I can admire other looks, but when I am shopping I don't even look at the other stuff, I can delete it all from my head. Floaty chiffon, huge prints, low-cut tops – nope. Life just got more relaxed.

School mornings are easy with the kids as they wear the same shirt, the same trousers and the same tie. Follow them. Get yours from John Lewis too if you want and stick to it. There's no heart-quickening in the shower I-have-a-meeting-what-should

-I-wear or who-do-I-want-to-be-today drama. Just pick and be done with it.

And, while we're here, if you do decide a fringe is for you, let me share what I have learnt. Have a long one (a short fringe has only worked for Larry Hagman and that's a fact) and have it trimmed once every three months (when it's overgrown it's good). Comb your hair in the shower after you've applied conditioner (I can be unbelievably boring about this) and don't use a hairdryer but just comb it into your eyes instead. Try to let it dry on its own and don't worry if the sides curl up. Don't use any product on it (especially not oil – I will never understand the 'I've just washed my hair and now I want it to look greasy' thing) and go about your business.

If your fringe is still jumping up and not behaving then go back to your hairdresser and ask for a heavier one. If you have curly hair it will have to be especially weighty. You don't want anything apologetic here. If it needs to start at the back of the head to gain heft then so be it. If it starts parting randomly in the middle then it's trim time. If none of the above works and you still want a curtain of hair on your forehead then it's time to invest in a straightening iron. Wash, let it dry naturally and then yank as much as you can and iron until it's a bulky field of mane. While it is unlikely that anyone will be able to see you clearly under there and they may describe you as 'the one who looks like an English Sheepdog' you now have a look. Good.

BRIDGE

Let's chat about reputations.

Let's start with me. We haven't met but I'd really like you to think that I'm cool, maybe a little naughty. That all the tatty dark t-shirts and black filthy eye make-up means I might be a right laugh, a fun person to have a night out with. That I probably stay out late, hammering on the piano in a private members' club at midnight while necking vodka. That's certainly the vibe I'm trying to give off.

I can tell you now I'm none of those things.

Bridge's rep, you could say, is also all wrong, a bit of a smokescreen. When I tell people I started playing in my 20s they look at me suspiciously. They think I might have got the right word but the wrong *meaning*. Do you mean you like to do gymnastics and create a bridge with your back after a couple of glasses of wine with the dancers from *Strictly*? Are you talking about extraordinary feats of civil engineering? Do you prefer a suspension, a truss or a cantilever?

When bridge the card game is mentioned it seems to conjure up for people images of old people, reading glasses round their neck, blanket on their lap, playing with a thimble of wine and some Ritz crackers. It's just not true. Bridge is – and this is a massive statement but I'm sticking by it – simply the greatest game in the world. It's not complicated, you don't have to be clever, you don't need to be good at maths (I'm numerically dyslexic, ask me to repeat a four-digit number back to you and I'll throw up on myself in panic) and you definitely don't need to be old.

The game consists of two parts – the bidding and the playing. I don't know if you like spy stories, unpicking clues. I'm not sure if you fancy the idea of being Poirot or Columbo for an evening, if you inhaled Agatha Christie novels, but if this ticks any of your boxes then you're going to absolutely adore the first round. No, you don't have to dress up, it's not a murder mystery party, no one needs to come to the table dressed as Colonel Mustard. Bidding is like being Bond (but less misogynistic and less interested in killing) as you and your bridge partner try to get to the perfect bid.

You go back and forth, you're talking to each other using only two words – for example, 'three hearts' or 'four clubs' – you can't give your hand away but through this coded chat you just might be able to work out if you can win this round. I'm not exaggerating when I say this is tense but terrifically addictive. There is no such thing as a bad hand in bridge. Whatever hand you're dealt you can handle – either by winning your bid or taking your opponents down. This is slow, it's stimulating, it's nail biting and you know that feeling before someone you really fancy kisses you? The butterflies and slight giddiness? It's like that. But there's no rejection, plus you're sitting down with snacks. Immediately better.

You find your bid. Everyone exhales. The next part is the play and this is nerve-wracking and completely exhilarating in equal measure. One of you will play, your partner's hand will be down on the table and here's the rub, the nugget, the zinger, you're a *team*. It is official bridge practice to say 'Good luck, partner' when you lay down your cards and your partner replies with a 'Thank you, partner.' Now, I don't want you to panic, you don't have to bow, you don't have to say it loudly but this really is the absolute joy of the game. The key word here is 'partner'. Without wanting to sound like a Spice Girl, two really do become one. You might be playing, your partner might be playing but you are doing it together. You don't win by yourself and, rather magically, you don't lose by yourself in bridge. Of course if you play particularly badly you feel sad about letting them down but you're not abseiling down a crevice in a torrential downpour, it's not life or death, it's just cards and they understand.

Bridge is about communication, it's about linking in with each other's head, it's about using a part of your brain that is often (in my case, always) dormant. It is easily the sexiest thing you can do on a night out. The thrill is seeing your cards, the flirtation is the bidding and then the build-up comes to the fore with the play.

Bridge is not stuffy, it's not for the over-70s. Find a bridge club and just start. If you don't love it after the first session I'll eat my Columbo hat. People talk about endorphins being released during exercise? This is a brain workout and you'll go to bed higher than a kite. Much better than actually getting high at the Groucho.

HOLIDAYS

I feel so strongly about holidays I have used subheadings. I know.

BOOKING

I know it's not cool, it's not relaxed, it's not attractive, but the truth is I like to be in control. When it comes to trips, I like to book. I want to choose where we go, how we get there and when we do it.

I nod while he says he'd like for us all to go to Sweden. I am doing a good job of ears closed listening (all women need this, it's a skill we have to pick up from men) and I really look like I'm considering it. I even mention getting a guide book. Meatballs in punnets and walking through the city all day? What a lovely plan. Staying in an Airbnb and then a trip to the Abba museum? I'm nodding vigorously now. After 22 years together, he still hasn't learnt that the more keen I appear, the less likely it is going to happen.

I actually whooped when he suggested going to the Secret Cinema once (dressing up and watching a film in a warehouse with other grown-ups all dressed up? Look, if you want to go to a swingers' party just say so) and he was surprised when the tickets never showed up. He's also convinced I seriously considered Ben Nevis in October, a pot-luck discovery car adventure with nothing booked in northern France and flying to South Africa on Christmas Day. He vaguely thinks that these things did not come to pass because something happened with expedia.com or I got some work (that I magically never went to) or there was a problem with getting rooms. (See also: anal sex, a homemade pizza oven – Dominos is up the road – and booking a sleepover for all of us in the bug house at the zoo). Super keen, yay, excellent, back of the net. Sure. Let's *definitely* do that.

Look, I know. Of course I *could* just tell him. But I don't want to be the naysayer, I don't want to be the boring one when the rest of the family is up for cinnamon buns and lingonberries in the home of IKEA. Plus, I don't really like confrontation – I actually often don't have time for confrontation – and I'd rather not use my energy on explaining why I don't want to do something. Smiling and nodding is simply the path of least resistance. Yes, of course baby. I would love to go to Tallinn for the weekend, I'll have a look tomorrow.

PACKING

There are a few things I can't stand – Ovaltine (a hot drink that smells of old socks but also develops a skin, are they nuts?), flying down a zip wire and people who tell you all about their dreams (save it). But the thing that I can't actually stomach is packing. I can't bear the stress, the counting of pants and the unending worry and panic about leaving stuff behind. On top of this, I am chronically, terribly, excoriatingly bad at it.

Here's an example. I've just got engaged. We've been together a year and, to be frank, we've spent at least 300 of those days in bed. I'm 26 and gaga about him. I'm so in love, I'm so awed by the sex (don't worry, my kids aren't reading this, they think everything I do is chronic) that we really have just spent a year under the covers on a futon with the papers and old pizza. I've met his parents but it's been brief. A few suppers, a Christmas Eve, a lot of smiling. I asked the right questions and we ate Danish food (gosh, herring three ways, *gesundheit*) and then we raced home again, tore our clothes off and got under the covers.

Now we are going to France for three days, which will be the first time I really get to know his mum. You'd have thought that packing for this would be straightforward, wouldn't you? Please believe me when I tell you I packed seven pairs of trousers (one of them had feathers attached – I can't talk about it), three roll-neck sweaters (it was July), absolutely no tops and two mismatched shoes. Even if I was packing in the dark, under intense time pressure, I should have done better. If I was on a game show called 'Packing in a Hurry' and Paddy McGuinness was standing over me yelling 'put it in the bag' and the crowd were going wild (whoever packs the best bag for the fishing expedition/Ice Hotel/Mongolia was going to win the holiday of a lifetime). Even THEN, I'd have done better. 'Aren't you warm?' came the casual question at the first breakfast when my future mother-in-law noticed I was wearing a mohair hoodie, suit trousers with one navy ballet flat and one black. There are no words.

And then of course there was the packing for the honeymoon. The destination was a surprise (have I told you he's very romantic? Total opposite of me) and he said he'd pack my bag for me. I checked it before we left. Only two swimsuits and a couple of kaftans and some flip flops. This bloke is having a laugh, this is surely a trick, I thought.

The problem was that I was completely sure I had 'sensed' where we were going (in the early days of the fringe I felt like Mystic Meg). I was certain he was taking me walking so at the last minute, I totally repacked and swapped the sun cream for walking boots and wind breakers and a flask. Yup, not very useful in Bali. I spent the full two weeks in a cagoule.

Whenever I've packed for the kids for a school trip there's always the call from the teacher on the first night: 'Good evening, I don't want to bother you but I was just wondering (I'm in a panic by now), do you happen to know if you packed Tilda's wellies?'

'Wellies? I thought you guys were going on a geography trip, I gave her some marshmallows and an atlas.'

'Well, yes, great but … it's extremely muddy.'

It's not like I don't have the stuff. We have the stuff. The rain macs, the goggles (well, we don't have these but I like to pretend I have an aquatic drawer also full of flippers) and we certainly have t-shirts and walking stuff and swimwear. So why can't I quite get the stuff in the bag?

I've never once been abroad and remembered to pack a plug convertor (I have three still in their packets) or a charger (so sorry, but can we stop off at Currys?) or the right toiletries (I seem to have glitter face paint, three of the same lipstick but absolutely no toothpaste or contact lenses) and nothing matches anything.

What is the secret to packing? I'm not asking for a friend, I'm asking for me. Do I need to write stuff down? I make lists – shoes, Mini Cheddars for the plane, some books, clothes – but they never, ever make it into the suitcase. Actually, I did once take cards but there were only fifty in the pack. *Bingo.*

THE AIRPORT

We wake up at 5am (why do I book planes at 8? Also confusing) and by the time we've checked in, gone through security there is then a heated debate about eating.

One of us wants sushi (it's early, you can't possibly want raw fish) and two others want toasties and I always like a pub at a terminal – can't explain why. We lose each other and the seventeen-year-old seems to inhale his boarding pass. We have to find a way to print him a new one as it transpires he's thrown it away in Smith's because he thought it was a receipt (yes, this is why he must never leave home) and then we either get to the gate with an hour to spare or at the last minute.

I want to be the kind of person who reserves a row of seats long before the flight leaves but this has never happened (I promise I'm organised in other ways – my books are ordered with Tetris-like precision) so we're all in middle seats and none of us are next to each other. So sorry do you mind moving? Sorry. Sorry. He's eight. Yes, I am that dickhead.

UNPACKING

This is an absolute disgrace. There are no drawers, there's a fight about two lone hangars that are attached to the rail and where to sleep.

'Why do I always get the camp bed? I'm six foot and he's tiny.'

'Where's my favourite teddy?' (Ah, I seem to remember last seeing Blue Cat in Heathrow).

Thankfully I've packed almost nothing or everything I've packed is completely unsuitable – 'Claud, how come you've brought knee-high boots and a puffa to Portugal?' Everything may as well stay in the suitcase and we go and discover the resort.

CREAMING

Can we talk about applying sun cream on small children? I don't know why it's more complicated than an obstacle course on the Krypton Factor but it is. First day you're up for it, you're ready. You've put some on yourself (ish) and now your sleeves are rolled up, bath mat is down and a little body is in front of you. This cannot, will not be the end of me. I can do this. It's cream, they just have to be covered so we don't have to stress-buy calamine lotion and put them in an ice bath. I'm really concentrating – arms, torso, back of the neck, nose, face (ah, sorry, yes some got in your eyes) and then the legs. I swear I love them and I'm focused. Always, without fail, at the end of the first day there's a large, angry red blotch somewhere that didn't get any. 'Mummy, it hurts if I get in the bath, ow, don't touch it.' Never mind, we'll just have to spend the next six days in the shade. Shit.

HELP, WHERE'S MY SPOT

Do we want to be by the pool? Should we try and go into town or get the bus to the beach? Where are we having lunch? How can they be hungry, it's 10.05? Everyone else in my family is relaxed. They're happy to throw down a towel and get a book and enjoy the day. Ah, here's an old broken deck chair and if I just get rid of these bottles of half-drunk water it'll be fine. This is lovely.

Uh, guys, there might be a better area, let's find it. Shall we walk round again and check we want to be here? They're all chilled (not my word) so I traipse around alone, battered by the sun, old sunglasses falling off my nose. I drop my book in the kids' pool and it takes ages to find my way back to them.

Now also starving. One of the kids has found and is tormenting a crab. Husband smiling and enjoying himself 'Hi babe, where have you been?' (Is there anything more infuriating?)

HELLO THERE!

I like people. I like making friends. I want to sit next to someone I don't know at dinner and find out all about them. Is it amazing being a grandpa? I see, you've just found out you're allergic to gluten, what do you eat for breakfast? I can do it, I can win awards at it, I genuinely like getting to know people and discovering a slice of their life. Stick me absolutely anywhere. My husband met someone new at work and we're going to the movies with him and his boyfriend. Fantastic. This is the way I live, that's how I roll. But not, I repeat, not, on holiday.

'Ah, is that book good?'

Excuse me? I'm lying on a lounger and have crisps on my chest. I have 30 minutes of golden time as the other four are walking down the beach. I'm listening to Britney Spears on my headphones, my nose is solidly in this book. Please, please tell me you're not talking to me. Ah, you are. Jesus, you've sat down. Do we all want to eat together tonight? In town? Somewhere that does dinner and a show and starts at 9?

Help. Me.

THE BUFFET

Every marriage is different and is tried and tested in different ways. He doesn't like her family/she loathes his friends/he likes drinking/she likes MDF (I'm not positive it's actually called that)/he wants four children/she daydreams about a dalmatian puppy. We're put through our paces and certain times will try us more than others.

I love a buffet. If it was up to me, this is how we'd always eat if we went out. A table laden with an assortment of things – some different breads, some cold hunks of cheese. Oh look! There's a curry. Hold on to your hats, is that an omelette station? I get so over-excited I forget to chat, to enjoy each other. I'm bobbing up and down from my seat. I've been known to get up again for a single melon ball (how do they do it? I marvelled for about thirty minutes).

My husband cannot cope with this. He thinks dinner or

lunch or breakfast out together is about chatting, sometimes flirting, finding out a bit more about each other (I mean, dude, there *is* nothing else). Not me. For me it's about looking at all the delicious things and then eating them in turn.

'That's nice darling, I never knew that happened when you were seven. Argh! The carvery has started. Back in a bit. Shall I get anyone some more poppyseed crispbread?' He likes a menu and a sit down, not a constant get up and sit down again. If there's a buffet, I'll try everything – wow, look at the lamb, it's wearing little hats. Soup at breakfast, I'm in. They're deep-frying risotto balls! He's appalled and would rather have a bowl of nuts on a bench. You see, there are many ways in which a marriage can be tested.

PACKING. AGAIN.

The sunburn has settled down, we found our perfect location and settled there every morning (massive umbrella to hand plus small stand for cream, headphones, phone – I am an arse), we were friendly to the couple but didn't have to be with them every second. The kids made friends, we established a buffet rotation so that sometimes we skipped it and chatted with crisps and fruit in our room instead. We found Monopoly at the front desk and all was good. And just as that magical unfurling happens it's time to pack again.

This time everything is sandy and damp and inside out. We bundle everything in our bags and there is no order. 'Sweetheart, shall we put all the dirty clothes in one bag and then the clean in the other?' Sure we can, but then I would think you're a psychopath. Your choice.

HOME

Our house is much smaller than we remembered. The post clogs the front door and we forgot to throw the milk away plus some old cheese is on the turn. You can now only open the fridge if you're wearing a snorkel. The bags stay in the hall for a week as nobody can face the sand and the damp. We're half a stone heavier than when we left, due to the buffets and the ice cream, and it's now back to real life.

I like holidays but I really, really like staying at home.

SHOULDERS

There are some wonderful things about getting older. I wouldn't be in my twenties again, they were too nervy, too angst-ridden. Am I coming across the right way? Am I holding this fork correctly? When will I have a baby? What will I do with my life? And then I think I spent most of my thirties pregnant or nursing and worrying about milk ducts and sleep schedules and nursery rhymes. But my forties have been great; my late forties even better.

You've just got used to your face, you've just worked out how to slow-cook a ham and you've finally decided where you like to be and what you like to do (for me, this is 'bed' and 'bridge', although not at the same time). If you've got kids, things are hopefully getting easier as they're older too and no longer waking up at 2, 4 and 6am.

Friendships are fully solid now. There aren't that many new ones coming in and, as a gang, we're not letting anyone leave. Yes, one of us will make mistakes – we forget to call back, we get too pickled, we're slightly self-obsessed – but we know it's just a phase, we have history and that's important. We've all been through proper stuff too. It's not just, 'I want to nick that lipstick and should I let him put his hand under my bra?' any more, it's deeper, it's more important.

We've dealt with death, pain, sadness – our parents are older, or some gone already; our kids have tested us; maybe some of us have realised we married turds. We've had the big chats, the why are we here, the 'I'm not happy' conversations and we've pulled each other out. Of course there's still drinking and howling and 'Should I get that jacket?' but it's multi-layered now, it's sometimes – actually often – profound.

If we're lucky, by the time we hit our mid-forties we will have more financial security. Or at least a better understanding of money and how to take charge of what we do have. We're old enough now to realise that a 900-quid coat is a bit of a nonsense and we're happy that we own a colander. We spend wisely (at least, most of the time), we know that splurging more on Jarlsberg and less on sparkly clutch bags is better. We can take great pride in the objects we've collected, whether that's an outstanding assortment of vases or ceramic bowls or a dazzling pile of high heels (remember when only having one pair of 'going-out shoes' was the norm? Now we have a choice. And we know how to avoid the ones that will shred our feet).

We've come to know and care about things that we didn't when we were 24. It might be the environment, it might be about equality, about protecting women's rights – maybe we volunteer for our local food bank or hospital. Some of us march, some of us raise money but we have a cause, something we care about (which isn't just ourselves or our small circle). We've come to realise that giving something back and being less selfish makes us feel better even than our fancy boots ever do.

And yet. I feel that alongside all of these advantages I should mention the effect of the ageing process on our bodies and our faces. Everything was springy once, everything was easy to handle; you could drink and eat whatever you wanted. You wanted to get into a tight dress on Saturday? Maybe skip lunch on Friday. Easy. Nothing to see here – just having some leaves and one olive so I can zip my jeans up. Age rather shits all over that. Your hormones mean that if you want to get into an unforgiving outfit on Saturday you will have to have juiced for three weeks prior. Your elastic face is, well, less elastic and whereas before a bit of lipstick and a big scarf meant you were dressed, this now looks a little tragic. It's somehow not enough. Wait, this used to work. I've put on clean clothes, some tinted moisturiser and am chewing gum, why do I still look like Meatloaf?

But I have good news. I have found the body part that, even in our late forties and beyond, we can really go to town with. Our necks are craggy and crumpled (this might just be me) and our knees are now made entirely of crepe. Bikinis are long gone as our stomachs are like an accordion made of skin. It doesn't matter whether you've done sit-ups (so don't bother), whether you're fat or thin, there are now dozens of weird little rolls that appear. But because we're older and know that eating and breaking bread and laughing with friends is vital, we refuse to pass up on cake or pizza or potatoes and all the other stuff that makes life great on a Thursday night.

So let me tell you about the area we can really focus on, the one that, for some miraculous reason, hasn't fallen apart. Shoulders. Bare shoulders can shrug (excellent, involves no words but this gesture says everything) and they can twinkle and glisten under good lights. Wear strapless anything, wear a sweater that falls off the shoulder, don stuff with a wide neckline that means the clavicle is showing. With shoulders out we can flirt, we can laugh (although try to avoid dislocation) and we can take all the good of getting old and still hold on to the 'Yeah, I'm going out and feel like an absolute sex god tonight.'

Don't worry about botox (I'm not surprised, this is just my new face) and avoid the expensive creams that do nothing (yes, I know the advertising is compelling but she's a supermodel and is 22) and don't give a stuff about your baggy knees. Just rely on the two bony bits on top of your arms either side of your neck. Shoulders and a sense of humour about the crumbling of everything else will get us through.

Quite

BIG

STRICTLY

This might be why you're here so here goes, let me divulge. If I haven't covered enough then I'm happy to answer any questions. Tweet me and I'll reply, that's the deal. You've got the book and you want to know what Giovanni looks like without his top on – I get it, just let me know. (By the way, if that is the question, the answer is knockout, plus much more muscular than you'd think.)

Strictly has been (I don't want your stomach to turn, so please be prepared) a gift to me. A barnstorming, stonking, thunderbolt of a present. I started working on *It Takes Two* in 2004. There had been one series already, my son was tiny and they said, 'Look, can you talk about the foxtrot every night live at 6.30pm?' I could be with him all morning and then go to work. I know. It was a six-week run and I was ridiculously lucky.

I then went on to present the results show and when Sir Bruce resigned I got Tess's job. Sometimes good fortune just falls in your lap. How did I, a short, scruffy, orange idiot get to be part of one of the nation's favourite TV shows? All I can say is that there has been no better example of right place, right time on earth. If you like watching it (I realise some of you won't), I'd like to tell you what it's like working on it.

———

The first day is the thrilling bit. This is when we get to find out who will be taking part. We get the list (everyone is given code names so their identities don't leak out – one year they were all cartoon characters and we used to have excellent conversations about whether Daffy Duck or Cinderella would dance first – magnificent) and once we've got the names then we can really start getting excited.

I should say that they tell me last minute after an 'incident' in 2006. You see, they told me early who was taking part and they'd given me everyone's bios. I was eager and ready to do my research (when I say 'research', I mean watch *EastEnders* for hours, getting on Wikipedia while holding a pen) and, on leaving the BBC, I jumped in the lift. Someone (friendly, smiley, rucksack) asked if I knew who was going to be in the cast. I rattled off the list and the next day he told everyone on his floor (not his fault, mine) and they decided that I was absolutely useless at keeping a secret. I'm pretty sure they now tell Tess weeks before me. I'm like a toddler with a dicky tummy – not good at keeping anything in.

We don't take it for granted that people will watch again every year. That would be stupid, and arrogant, and deeply uncool. At the launch, there's anticipation in the air: will they watch, will they come, will anybody care? We're also desperate to see these humans move. Can they dance? Can they clap in time? (I can't, incidentally) and will they gel with everyone else (they do). But mainly there's the fear – a real deep-down sense of 'Help, what if people don't want to watch it anymore?' This is healthy and normal but it's a great relief when the studio audience is happy to see everyone. They love the professional dancers so much. One group dance and we're on our way.

When we are getting ready to start filming, I always have the same problem. It's this – from January until the end of August I wear exactly the same thing: black jeans, black sweater and boots and my body is wholly covered up. Maybe there's a fortnight away but obviously I stay in the shade in a massive t-shirt (my skin no longer recognises the actual sun, it only accepts tan if it's from Boots). Your human bulk gets bigger, it gets smaller, no biggie. Sometimes it's in the mood for pizza, sometimes it wants to order cous cous (I've actually never ordered cous cous, it's a disgrace, but you get the picture). Either way, throughout these months, my physical self, if you will, is not really my concern. I don't have a full-length mirror at home so I am never really engaged in my physique.

Then all of a sudden it's *Strictly* season and I need to be aware of the stuff that's going on below my neck. I should be used to this by now, this should be calculated, and yet every year it's still a surprise. Oh, legs out you say? They want me in bright green? I need to think about floor-length gowns (help) and thigh slits and Spanx (might need to wear two pairs) and all that jazz.

Thankfully, a brilliant human being called Sinead helps. We spend a day out trying to buy anything glitzy that will fit and that I can walk in. My preference would be to get one black suit and wear it every week (possibly with slightly different sized gold hoop earrings) but this is not enough I've been told. Come on, make an effort, wear some colour, do it. They're not wrong. While constantly wearing black in real life is sensible and effective (see page 191), on TV it looks lazy. It's a cold night in November and the kind viewers who are keeping us in jobs deserve scarlet, electric blue, bright yellow. Just trundling onto an entertainment show in a black t-shirt is aloof, very much not in the spirit of it all.

It's actually a privilege to get all dressed up and wear these clothes. We don't keep them, of course – the BBC will reuse everything again and again. One long pink dress from 2012 has been on soaps, dramas and three other entertainment shows and this makes me happy. We buy and pass on and eventually the dresses Tess and I wear will be sold and the money goes to charity.

Because of this important fact, because they're never actually ending up in my wardrobe, we can go a bit more nuts, be slightly braver. We're not buying anything that needs to be for life, it just needs to be for once. It needs to be for *Strictly*. A full gold sequin trouser suit? With gold platforms and a gold choker? Are you sure? Is it too much? Yes. Then definitely add to basket. A silver bejewelled *and* lamé zebra-print dress? Let's take it to the till.

Less is simply less on *Strictly*. You think that fully beaded rainbow yeti dress is a little bit too musicals, too out there, too overdone? Yes, you're right. It'll be perfect. Basically, I'm going to the best fancy dress party every Saturday night for twelve weeks in a row and I love every second. And then at the drinks after the final I am back in the same black jeans, the same old boots and won't take them off for eight months. Sorted.

You never get used to the nerves. Everything is fine, everything is prepared – that's what I tell myself. We've rehearsed; when I practised the autocue script I didn't trip up over 'the scores are in'. Good. I'm fully 'done' (hair, make-up, clothes) and have said good luck to the couples who are quaking behind the sparkly curtain. It's a few minutes to lights up, to being live on air, and suddenly my mouth goes funny. I'm actually not quite sure I can speak – god, why is it so dry? Why has my tongue doubled in size? Quick, have another swig of Diet 7up (I should explain I don't really 'do' water – it's too showy, too healthy, too pleased with itself) and we say hello to the audience. They're charming, they're ready, they're excited. We're terrified, please help us we say, please support the dancers we plead.

I have to slightly punch Tess (I promise it's not a real punch, more of a nudge) to try to get rid of the nerves but they come anyway. They mount and when there's 30 seconds to go, it's like I'm under a massive wave of hysteria. Yes, it's only telly and sure, it doesn't really matter in the grand scheme of things if I fall over or mess up the words, I know we'd all survive. I'm hardly in an operating theatre holding a scalpel. But the sense of responsibility and not wanting to let everyone down still feels huge.

Strictly is a large, often long, complicated show and the brilliant director is spinning hundreds of plates. We presenters are only tiny cogs in an enormous machine. Many components need to fit into the time slot – the band need to be showcased, the dances have to have enough time, the judges should be allowed to give a full assessment and in order for this to happen we have to hit our timings. Wanging on in the hello or going off piste in a chat is selfish and puts everything else out.

More breathing (trying) and then that's it, the floor manager has nudged me under the light. I'm holding onto Anton or Gorka or Johannes and it's time, the theme tune is playing and I'm walking (I'm not sure how) and we're on air and I could be sick and I feel slightly queasy knowing I could do the wrong thing – if I bugger it up, if I swear, if I fall over, if I can't see the words, if I introduce the wrong thing. The entity that's keeping me stable and solid, that means I'm able to stay on the right spot (if I'm really swaying it means I'm terrified btw), is Tess, who's like a beautiful, blonde, kind anchor.

The studio audience are clapping; I can hear a 'cue' in my earpiece and, to be frank, this is the deal, this is the job. I can bond with the dancers and the celebs and I can bring in cookies for the script reads but I've basically been hired to look down the barrel of the lens and say the words in front of me. It sounds easy. Some good news. It is.

Tess and I do some talking and then the dancing starts. I should be used to it. I should be immune, it's been sixteen years. Another Argentine tango? Whatever, I'm just over here eating a bun – you carry on. That is, however, just not how it is. The minute they dance and they love it (the key is that the ones who love it the most make the final – true fact) we all get goosebumps. I'm an old lady with hormones all over the place so I am used to feeling moved, so don't just take it from me. The camera crew, the props boys, the extraordinary producers – we all quite simply … go. If it's upbeat we move our little feet and clap along (or try to, in my case) and if it's emotional, moving and the band are playing (I should mention the wonder that is Dave Arch here) then that's it. We're hooked.

The celebrities are terrified too, they're the stars and they're totally out of their comfort zones. We get to know them, we know their kids' names, we tell them it will be OK, we try and look after them as best we can. They work so hard all week to perfect the dance and then when it goes well the room erupts and we celebrate with them. When the judges get out a 10 the excitement is real. We're not *laissez faire*, we're not all taking it in our stride. It might sound stupid but for that moment, for that couple, so often for their families, it matters.

After twelve weeks of pizza (Tess has pineapple on hers, apart from that fact she is a completely perfect human being) and dancing and fear it's all over and one will be crowned winner. The excellent team who make the show all dance and drink and we cuddle them and thank them and say (hopefully) see you next year. We leave on a high, we skip home covered in glitter and hair spray and an outrageous amount of fake tan, and yet the final is not the highlight for me. Weird but true.

You see, we go to Blackpool every year in November. It's bitterly cold and we take a couple of trains on the Thursday night or arrive slightly car-sick. Much of the pleasure beach is closed, the bed and breakfasts are 8 per cent full and the sea wind (it's not 'air' in November, it'll whip your hair up into a twisted pylon if you're outside for a minute) is fierce. If we were talking about any other town, any other location on earth it would probably be sad, slightly miserable, a bit of a let down. Leaving your families and cosy beds behind to meet at the seaside in the freezing rain? Here's the thing, though – it's Blackpool and I've never been to anywhere more welcoming in my life (no exaggeration). We love it there and they seem to love us.

Everyone has a massive smile – come and try my fish and chips; we have rock but it's not the kind that'll break your teeth as we make it fresh. Have dinner in this Thai restaurant, check out our noodles, better than London (they are). And then we all feel sad (and hungover, it has to be said) when we leave on Sunday. We'd film there every week if we were allowed.

We could all learn a little from Blackpool, actually. Kind, open arms, share our stuff, enjoy what we have. It's one of a kind. I have no idea what it's like in the summer but in the depths of winter when it gets dark at 4 and the whole place is covered in a gentle drizzle – it's pure magic.

BEING WRONG

I am 48 years old and I've got to the age when I think I know things. I've decided what sort of restaurants I like, what kind of people I like, what kind of music I like. I'm deeply proud of my just 'knowing'.

'Babe, shall we try that new poke place?' Nope. I don't like it. It's just chopped stuff on cold rice, don't get it, we'll have Lebanese food instead.

'Claud, shall we go with green eye shadow for tonight's show?' Have you got a temperature? Did you bang your head? The only colour I'll accept is black, maybe navy on special occasions.

'Mum, instead of a holiday by ourselves shall we go away with friends?' Afraid not pumpkin, I have no interest in going away with you only to spend no time with you. I don't like getting drunk with other grown-ups at lunch enough, you see. I like it when it's just us family, a lot of chatting and Bird Bingo.

I am also extremely proud of my love of concrete. I have spent the last 48 years (give or take – for the first five I didn't have a full-on opinion) believing that city life was the only life. I live on a bus lane, I like noise, I am in love with sushi and I always need to be near a 24-hour chemist. I like cinemas and bustle and traffic and hooting. I like odd smells that waft out of restaurant basements and I relish in the London underground.

Embarrassingly, I've always been even slightly emotional about it. The tube got me to school every day aged 7–18, it got me out of tricky situations (you never need to stay with a boy on the turn when the Northern Line is on offer) and now it whizzes my kids about to school, to friends' houses. Plus it's never, ever cold (this is key).

I like eating on a busy street – a bagel surrounded by fumes is joyful – I like pigeons and I really like that a selection of movie start times are on offer in various cinemas across the city. I like deciding to eat Thai food at 7:56pm and then eating it at 8:19. I like options. Look at all those little wine shops next to each other, let's go to a different one every Friday. Good. That makes sense.

Like so many 'solutions' I'd come to, my adoration for city life was pretty clear cut, it was sewn up, it was done. I could never comprehend living in a village that had one pub, a lone bench and possibly a post box. Friends though, one by one, slowly moved to the countryside.

Once they'd made the decision to go, they'd sit me down, assuring me I should not take it personally (I did), and they'd talk about better schools, mention 'oxygen' (no, not sure) and announce that they'd apparently been dreaming of vegetable patches and space (what?). They'd declare their need for a dog and Sunday lunches and walks and fresh eggs. Yawn.

Of course, in return, I'd make (I thought) quite a strong case for cramped flats and pollution and hullabaloo. I'd tell them that dogs defecated (you simply can't get away from it) and I'd reassure them that my local Tesco Metro did indeed sell eggs. And that yes, I was completely certain they were fresh. The conversation would always end with them patting me on the shoulder pityingly. They said I was a bit sad, a bit stuck and a bit mistaken. They said I was like the last person at the party who hasn't noticed that everyone has already left. I was the woman in the kitchen shouting 'one more shot' to absolutely nobody as the last guests were already on their way out the front door.

I let them go (turns out you can't actually kidnap friends) and looked forward to them calling, sobbing down the phone about creepy neighbours, the endless spiderwebs, the village green being a hotbed of gossip. I couldn't wait to hear all about how they needed their hair done, their nails done, their eyebrows done and how they just couldn't. I waited to see how they liked living looking like the Gruffalo. I was envisaging hilarious chats, where I would say, 'Send me photos!' And, 'Ha ha. You're feral!'

Every time my phone buzzed I'd think, 'Here we go, they're coming back. They've missed bars and taxis and Pret. How can they survive without Deliveroo? Babe, put the kettle on, this'll be them now. I should probably start looking for a flat for them. There's one available just on that busy intersection between the petrol station and the supermarket. It'll be small, damp, overpriced and the lift is likely dodgy but they'll be able to buy a Twix at 3am. Better.'

Here's the thing – the calls never came. They didn't cry, they didn't hate the village green, some of them even entered vegetable and cake competitions and their kids put their phones away, removed their belly button piercings and took up knitting and books and tennis. I'd text, 'You OK?' and get a message back, simply saying 'Great!' with a photo of a sheep or a beautifully set table in the garden or a blue sky. They were enjoying the marrow planting too much to worry about nails and hair and spray tans. They'd, gulp, moved on.

I finally went to visit.

'Come, you have to come! Just get in the car.'

'I don't have a car.'

'You do have a car. I've seen it. Come! Wait till you see my tomatoes, wait till you meet the dog, wait till you see our garden, we've got a trampoline!'

Livid, I went to investigate. I wore completely inappropriate clothing to make a point (overly tight skinny jeans, pointy boots, absolutely nothing in racing green or, god forbid, brown) and went to see a friend who lives in an actual field. 'Can you *imagine?*' I said to my husband, as we arrived and parked next to a real-life ditch.

Now, wait just a second. Everyone hold your horses (well, when I say 'everyone' I mean me and yes, they have them there). The countryside is not what I thought it was. There were trees and stuff to pick from them. Don't quiz me on what, if it's not wrapped in cellophane and labelled I'm not completely sure what it is. We talked to chickens. We ate lunch that wasn't just a whole sheep crammed in an Aga (that's pretty much what I thought food was outside the M25) and we went for a walk. We weren't walking *to a place*, you understand. We weren't getting anything, we weren't going to pick something up, we were just, well, having a walk. It was, drumroll please … absolutely outstanding.

The countryside is bloody fantastic. It's green, there's space, there are fields, there are animals just wandering about (we walked past three cows). My kids loved the trampoline (the only one they'd ever seen was in a concrete hangar in Acton) and we ate local cheese (what does that even mean?) and fed ducks in a genuine pond.

Don't panic, I'm not leaving my beloved city streets, I'm still picking up sushi at 9pm and I will never be far from the Central Line. But, still, the whole experience was an excellent reminder and a great leveller because it showed me this: it is absolutely brilliant being wrong. There's something fabulously freeing when you realise you don't really know anything at all. Perhaps (and I mean definitely) I'm wrong about all kinds of stuff – those strongly held beliefs might just be puffs of smoke, a rigid, desperate hold on opinions that are nonsense. So yes, maybe let's try that poke place, let's consider going away with our mates and maybe I'll even give green eye shadow a go. (Don't worry, I'm kidding about the last one.)

FRIENDSHIP

Right then. Here, I suppose, is the nub of the 'book' (yes, I'm using inverted commas). When I was thinking about all I wanted to say and wang on about, it basically came down to this, to friends. Of course I also wanted to mention pirate boots, fondue sets, yoga, coconut yoghurt, personalised number plates, people over the age of ten who seriously enquire if you're a Sagittarius and parents who own laminating machines. But I really wanted to write about friendship as girlfriends matter more than anything.

There are many different kinds and the truth is we need and should try to have them all. I want to point out friendship doesn't always come easily, it has to be nurtured and looked after and cherished. Friendship takes effort and attention, you can't expect it just to appear, we don't just 'deserve' great friends, we need to earn them. You know all that time we spent on 'I wonder if he'll like this top more than that top?' and 'I think lamb chops will seal the deal, how will he resist me once he's had these covered in my mustard chilli rub?'.

All that time on the men in our lives, from ones you fancy to long-term boyfriends and then husbands? Well the truth is men will come and go and children, if you've brought them up correctly, will one day confidently leave and start their own families (I can't believe I'm writing this, see page 234) but friends are for ever. Search for the right ones, fit round them, hold on to them tightly and don't let them go.

THE WILD ONE

I'd like everyone to have one of these. She creates fun and doesn't just expect and wait for it. Sure, she flirts with the waiter and shrieks a bit too loudly. She orders everything off the menu and she will suddenly decide that yes, even though you're in Camden and it's 11pm the party in Essex sounds like a great idea and if you don't want to come along she'll disappear faster than Keyser Söze. 'Bye, it was great. See you soon.'

She's crazier than you, she's got more energy than you, she's more fun than you. You don't want to go out, you try to cancel, you blame the traffic, the weather, your bank balance and she just won't have it. She marches through life, singing loudly, dancing when others aren't and drinking more than most. A Wetherspoons off the A40 that's 80 per cent empty on a Monday in January? With her it'll be better than a top-table seat at the Met Ball.

She's the last one standing and everyone loves her. She is the positive force in your friendship group who will rally everyone together. 'I know it's hailing but we said we'd meet/chat/drink so come on, it's in the sodding diary, see you at 8! Yes, we've *all* got bloody work tomorrow, deal with it. Four tequila shots, extra limes please and another bowl of chips.'

She's not the first person you call in a crisis, she's not that interested in the minutiae of your life (don't be offended, it's not just you, it's everyone) and she sometimes forgets how old your kids are. He's seventeen? I could swear he was ten. He loves Man U, right? Oh, Arsenal. Shame. But she's generous and vivacious and will lift a whole bar up if it's feeling blue.

Everyone needs one of these friends. Find her, don't cancel on her and always follow her on New Year's Eve as it's a hideous night full of ghastly high expectations but she'll make anything fun. Stuck outside a club which won't let you in? At a limp house party miles away from home? Your other friends would slump and complain and bring everything down. Not this one.

Hold on to her and share her happily with everyone – don't be jealous if she's into someone else right now, possessiveness doesn't work with her, she finds it spectacularly uncool. She'll go through life mingling with all sorts of groups. You never understand where she gets the energy from, she's a fizz bomb, a cracking firework of a human. She might sleep in on your wedding day and miss the ceremony (my friend did this) and she'll almost certainly have sex with your cousin if you take her on a family holiday to Wales (no comment) but don't blame her, she can't help it. Without her, life is a little less colourful.

THE ONE TWO STEPS IN FRONT OF YOU

She's a best friend but she's also a mentor. Her kids are older, she's been with her partner forever and maybe split up with him a couple of times, she bought a flat about five years before you. She's the one you call when you don't know whether to take the job in Edinburgh, when you're not sure if it's chickenpox, when you think your husband might be sleeping with someone at the office (why the hell has he got a new gym membership and what's with the colourful socks?). She has seen and knows it all.

She's not preachy, she doesn't insist that you must do this or that, she just has the knowledge and she's happy to hand it out. The little things – argh, his boss is coming over last minute and he's gluten free, what do I cook? Should I think about changing gas providers? How many fairy lights is too much? I want to send a thank you, how much do I spend on flowers? Do I add an X at the end of the text to his teacher if he gave her an A? Should I be taking hormones? She knows. The kids want a dog, we don't have a garden, is this a good idea? She has the answer, the breed and the best time to get one. I don't want/ can't afford a nanny but I can't do everything, what do I do? He only wants to have sex in the mornings but I've got to make three packed lunches.

This person is all-important. She's funny, she's been there, she's calm, she's the font of all knowledge. Gather her pieces of advice like hunks of gold and of course mould them to fit your life. She's like your mum, but less so.

And then it's your job to guide someone else who's a couple of steps behind you. All this wise advice she has at her fingertips was once given to her by someone more experienced; she passes it to you and you will pass it down to someone else. It's a sort of ladder of women, so to speak.

THE ONE WHO RAISES YOUR GAME

Everyone needs a great friend who's smarter than them. This friend pushes your brain boundaries, she suggests books that you think look like heavy going. She wants to meet up but she doesn't fancy Leon and a walk round Topshop, she wants to go to the new exhibition at least two tube changes away. She invites you to join her on marches and doesn't accept, 'But I'm sleepy, can't I sign a petition and donate instead?'

Her cultural references have moved on and deepened since college and it's not enough to just rely on Nietzsche and Sylvia Plath: 'Are you still talking about *The Bell Jar*, Claud? You read that over 30 years ago.' She inhales the culture supplement and sends screenshots over to you on a Sunday morning. All you want to read about is the latest mascara that promises to add both length *and* volume and she thinks you should both go to the Southbank for a talk about the future of digital photography. She makes your brain swell and she's deeply uninterested in celebrity gossip. You can tell her the names of Katie Price's children (and ages) but she wants to know how you feel about the Hilary Mantel trilogy and it's got to be better thought out than 'great'.

This is the friend who will stop you in your tracks and force you to go a little bit deeper. She's inquisitive and hasn't just settled. Everyone needs this friend. Sometimes you'll roll your eyes and say, 'But why can't we get a pizza and watch *Gogglebox*?' and the truth is she's happy to do that too. But then she'll insist you watch a subtitled film you've never heard of and aren't quite sure you can spell. Every time you leave the poetry reading/exhibition/theatre you're so grateful to have her in your life and often find yourself saying, 'I'd never have done that/watched that/read that/thought that. Thank you.'

THE SOUL MATE

If you're really lucky you'll meet her early and you'll just know. I did. I was 23 and sat opposite her and just thought, 'Wow, you're *the one*.' This person knows you much better than you know yourself. She'll spear someone in the eye if they hurt you and she understands every little section of your heart and your mind.

She sees your family, the way you were brought up, she watches the way you parent, she observes how you are with your partner. The greatest thing is that she holds absolutely no judgement. You can get too drunk in front of her, you can cancel her at the last minute and you can laugh and cry about almost nothing. You're there for her, you'd do anything to make her happy and she's there for you. Simply put, you're each other's best friends.

There's no hierarchy, there's no worry about asking for too much or giving too little. She's fair weather and great weather and is just your person. She gets you, the real you, she understands the good and the bad and takes it all. She wants you to have a good time but can also say, 'Be at mine early, hand round crisps, look after my uncle,' and it's no imposition. You have each other's backs and when the kids leave (why do I keep mentioning this?) you know you'll get through it, you'll survive it if she's right there with you. Your partner will have to understand it and if they're smart they'll love her too. If they don't, you won't question her, you'll question him.

THE NOSTALGIC ONE

You need a friend who was there when you first started. Would you be great friends with them if you met them now? Do they do the same things you do? Are they interested in the same things you are? Maybe not, but you've been friends forever so it doesn't really matter.

You were inseparable at school; maybe your parents were best friends so you had every holiday in Llandudno together from the age of four. It's extremely comforting to have a friend who knows your childhood inside out. They were there when your siblings were tiny, they know about the rows at Grandma's/Easter/on a camping trip. It's lovely to be friends with someone when you don't have to fill in the gaps. 'Well, you see, we always had chilli con carne at Christmas because ...' – none of that needs to happen. Seeing her reminds you of when you were both little, or perhaps the first time you both kissed a boy (in my case it was the same one – a very 'enthusiastic' night in Chalk Farm in the 80s) and you share a fantastic shorthand. All those maths lessons (she could do it, you could not), all those giggling fits in assembly, all those school trips and the time you threw up on the coach. You have history and that's compelling.

Being with her feels like coming home. Don't worry if you can only see her sporadically but always be there for her at the end of the phone, like she is with you. As your uncles and aunts and parents get older you'll want to reminisce with someone who was there, who remembers, and she'll want the same.

THE GROWN-UP

To balance the chaos created by the wild one(s) in the gang, every friendship group needs a fully fledged grown-up. The one who says things like, 'Girls, I know we're going to the party but I've pre-booked a cab to pick us up at 11 as it's a weekday,' and, 'I realise you want the Balenciaga bag but do you really, though? I mean, it's got a logo on it which is a bit naff and, I mean, have you seen the price? Why don't you live without it?' and, 'I realise you want a puppy, you keep asking everyone about it but you really don't have the space so it's cruel, I don't care what anyone else says.'

She's rarely drunk, she doesn't flirt, she can be quite serious and she asked for a crochet set for her 21st. She's the moral compass of the gang. If you want to do something naughty you absolutely don't call her. If you want to do something naughty and know you need to be talked down you absolutely call her.

She hates drugs and thinks caffeine after 4 is as dangerous as free-climbing in Utah. She tells you to go home when you start repeating yourself and she tells you to stop smiling at the man with the girlfriend. She's not boring, she's not faking, she just believes in an early night and being well behaved. She rather loves the fact that everyone worries about upsetting her. 'Don't do it, she'll disapprove' holds a certain kind of power. We all look to her to check we're not going too far, not annoying the people in the seats next to us. Nobody is late for her and everyone wants to make her happy. She's solid, she never cancels and she loves everyone equally. She's the reassuring presence, she's extremely kind and she's in charge of the line. She tells us when we're crossing it and nothing is worth her wrath.

I'd love to think I'm the wild one, the fun one, the naughty one but I've called my girls and here's some interesting news. This one apparently is me. And, while we're here, I'd just like to say caffeine really *is* quite risky after 4 and staying out after 11pm on a school night is simply reckless.

THE BIT TOO HONEST FRIEND

You don't really look forward to seeing her but are always grateful when you have. When you've left her you sometimes feel like you've been through a spin in the tumble dryer. She's unfailingly honest. Hand on heart fake sincerity is chronic (see page 221) but sometimes real honesty is important. It's good to sit opposite someone who's just going to tell you how it is. She's not at all worried about hurting your feelings, telling you that you're wrong, bringing you back down to earth.

'Why are you still presenting that show about dancing? You're way too orange on it.' 'Why are you still living in that house? You've been there for fifteen years and it's crumbling,' and 'I think your kids are fine but So-and-so's are just doing better.'

It's a real battering but is somehow cleansing. It isn't just a 'let's catch up' and 'well done' and 'gosh, is that bag new?' She's been in your life for a while and you don't really want to cut it off. You don't know why she feels the need to really stride along the truthful path but it's a bit like a fast, a quick detox. You know nothing is going to be sugar coated or surface-layer fun.

She'll tell you if your husband is being a tool, if you've invested in the wrong coat, if you're too over-protective, not protective enough. She'll tell you to stop cooking the same goddamn roast chicken every time she comes over and she'll tell you that you're too old to wear white stilettos (I've ignored this piece of advice). She'll question why you said yes to that party and no to the other one. She's completely and utterly forthright like nobody else is in your life. She can be brutal but she makes you think about your actions. Your catch-ups aren't shallow or flippant. She gets to the nub, you take it and then you walk home feeling like you've just had a personality peel. And at any age (but especially when you get older) this is a good thing.

SPORTS DAY

There are some experiences that bring out the very best in us. Firework displays – 'Come to the front, can you see?' Why don't I put your son on my shoulders so he can get a proper look? A new arrival – 'Give me your address, I can send clothes and books and would you like me to pop in and watch her while you have a shower or nap?' A break-up (my friends call it a state of emergency) – 'We're coming round, I've got crisps, of course you should throw his toothbrush in the bin, let's get drunk and get you on Tinder.' We come to the fore as a species at these times.

There are also some situations in which we do not, generally, show our nobler sides. When, in fact, we go slightly nuts. I'm talking about the first day of the sales – 'Sorry, I was here first and I really want new bedding.' In terrible traffic normally very gracious and serene people start screaming and swearing if the person in front of them is a little slow when the lights change. 'PUT YOUR FOOT ON THE PEDAL YOU ABSOLUTE ARSEWIPE' erupts out of our mouths from absolutely nowhere. We lose it during summer in general (see page 37) but the real biggie, when all the toys come out of the pram, when we don't recognise ourselves any more, usually involves a sack race.

Parenting is lovely, but it's also challenging sometimes, it ebbs and flows. We try our best and we understand we get things wrong and try not to beat ourselves up. We take Billy to school late; we forget that Ruby had to create the Milky Way using only some corn flakes and a tennis ball and we apologise to the teacher who nods sympathetically. We remember to test them on their spellings but only when we're nearly at the school gates; we throw some Wotsits and a bit of old ham in a paper bag for their lunch. We get by.

But there's one day of the year when all of this acceptance and managing and 'I think, I hope, I've done enough' goes up in smoke. When even the most relaxed parent loses their mind. It's not the run up to SATs. It's not the casting of the nativity. It's not even the frenzied day of the 11+. What I'm talking about here is sports day.

It is simply the weirdest day of the year. In the run-up, there's a low-level panic at the school gates. 'Are you practising, Claud? Remember there's the mum's race at 3! Don't blame your dicky knee this time! I've still got my medal on the fridge from two years ago. Just the feeling of the wind in my hair and crossing that finishing line still makes me giddy. And honestly, he still talks about it! "Mummy, you were the fastest out of all the mums!"'

'You really must start training you know, a simple stretch will do it and maybe a little jog before you go to the office. Also, can I strongly suggest more fibre in the lead up and maybe a light protein-filled breakfast on the day so you're not weighted down? We opt for boiled eggs and gluten-free seeded thins but you must do whatever you think best.'

The class WhatsApp group is normally a place of calm, a good hub to ask for help. 'Anyone got the maths homework?' 'Shit, World Book Day is coming up, I'm going to say he's ill – you?' 'Do they have to do the optional thing in science? I mean, it says optional.' Suddenly, a couple of weeks before sports day, it's taken over by savages. The chat is all, 'Is Zach practising? Molly isn't. I should also say her right calf is a bit off, bad fall at the park trying to see a duckling, so you know, don't expect much.' And, 'What lunch are you bringing? I'm thinking of just chucking some stuff together really. You know, some poached salmon. Maybe some banana bread. No biggie.'

The mums who are lovely and straightforward and together all suddenly lose it. And they're not alone – I'm not getting all judgy here, I go the most loopy of all. 'Kids, do we have enough golden syrup? I need to make flapjacks, but not the sticky, gunky ones we like to eat out of the pan – these need to be special. Quick, someone go to the shop to get some sesame seeds so I can toast them for the top. I'll say it's an Ottolenghi recipe. RUN!'

Sports day is the only day where the British suddenly lose our whole, 'Oh god, I'm absolutely shite' ethos that makes us who we are. The rest of the year it's all, 'Yeah, I made that quiche but it's completely disgusting, don't touch it.' 'This ancient thing I'm wearing? Think it's H&M from 2010, just found it lying under the dead moths at the back of the cupboard, yes, it's got ketchup on it.' Then one afternoon in late June or July, our fantastic underplaying of everything, our habitual total humility, our 'Please don't look at me, I'm seriously going to fail' is thrown to one side and parents go stark raving mad.

I am not sporty (the last time I wore leggings was in 2008 and that was by mistake) and my kids aren't particularly either. On the occasions they've said they'd like to give cricket a go I've tended to treat it with the same incredulousness as if they'd suddenly asked to learn how to play the French horn. But on this day, all the usual normalcy of life is thrown in the air and people – me very much included – find ourselves screaming, 'Take him, you moron!' from the sidelines.

Egg and spoon? I'm casual about it the night before and then it's the day itself and they're all standing there on the starting line. He's eight but surely he can do this. I mean, if he can't focus and keep it together and bloody win then how's he going to find a wife or a husband? How's he going to make a tuna bake? How's he going to survive? I'm sweating now (I don't know whether you've ever seen someone who wears as much fake tan as me perspiring but you should know it's grotesque) and I'm yelling at the top of my voice. 'Look forward, do NOT look at the spoon.' I'm hurling parents out of the way so I can video the whole thing (I will never look at this video again, by the way) and I'm losing my voice as I'm shouting, 'You can beat that bastard! Crush him!' My husband is cantering alongside him in a crab pose mouthing the words 'We believe in you' and our son comes second to last.

We brush off the mania and he tries to throw a bean bag into a bucket ('Focus puppy, stop looking at us') and then it's lunchtime. Do you know what I like for lunch? My absolute dream midday meal would be an egg sandwich, maybe a small soup, a handful (a giant's hand if you please) of Twiglets and a sparkly diet drink. It's not Michelin star, it's not anything worthy of more than a nod. On sports day I try to morph into Martha Stewart. I speak too loudly as I lay out the rug – 'We have extra buckwheat salads if anyone wants one … ' I don't even know what buckwheat *is*.

There is also a major and completely unspoken 'who's the best recycler' award which is being secretly fought for. Boxes made of dung anyone? 'Who needs a bamboo straw?' some-one yelps. Twice. We eat and then there's the makeshift cake stand. Again, left to my own devices I'd always pick a chunky KitKat. Here, there's enough nut-free, three-tiered cakes to kill an army. 'So, those are edible bluebells, we picked them our-selves!' 'You must try our plant-based jammy dodgers – what *did* we do before coconut sugar?!'

Then a few more races and home and everyone immediately goes back to normal again. A bit like a terrible drunken night with your friend and those two blokes you met at the bus sta-tion in 1994 – it simply never happened. The next day it's all, 'I'm giving him beans on toast every night this week, yeah, and they'll be cold' and, 'Does anyone have their history assign-ment? Aren't the Aztecs the same as the Incas?' Much better, much easier to navigate.

THE TUBE

Have you been to Rio? No, I'm not flirting. It's a genuine question.

If you have, you'll know it's very simply one of the greatest cities on earth. Let me describe – towering mountains, breath-taking beaches, insane hospitality. You'll be having dinner, the most delicious hot melting cheese puffs and miniature freezing cold beers and small marmosets might just join you. That's right, marmosets. Just on a regular side street. I spent some time there in 2013 and fell deeply in love with it; I'd literally never been anywhere like Rio.

But would I move there? Could I consider leaving my beloved London? I realise 'beloved' is a strong word – maybe you're thinking I live in a unique and gentrified area? Somewhere with a hot tub, extra clean air and blossom trees? I don't. I live in the middle – no garden and full-time concrete. It's excellent. I'm afraid I couldn't consider leaving because of one simple problem. In Rio, there isn't a tube.

I love so many things about London – the parks, the museums, the food, the people, the galleries. And the reason we can get to all of the above and more is because of the wonder that is the London underground.

My infatuation with the maze of primary-coloured stalks started when I was small. My parents called the tube 'the magic train' and whisked me everywhere on it, to museums, to parties, to aunts and uncles. It was a route to adventure, to novelty and often to too much cake.

As a teenager it was my place of deception. I'd leave home looking prim. Yes, my skirt is a respectable length, of course I won't wear make-up, I'm fully intending to check my history homework once I'm on the Northern Line and naturally I'll wear my glasses. Twelve minutes later I'd be in a tunnel hiking my skirt up and putting on mascara with friends.

Between Camden and Moorgate I'd get rid of the sensible ponytail and backcomb my hair until it was on stalks. In went the hoop earrings, in went the crispy contact lenses (I constantly had an eye infection) and on went the bright white lipstick and bingo, I was ready for the school day.

I'm not sure if you've spent much time on the tube, but the people who work for TFL are excessively kind. They also have an encyclopaedic knowledge of every single station. You're at Lancaster Gate and want to get to Blackfriars. 'There are two ways, one involves a lovely escalator that's just been done and the other has stairs but a gorgeous orange tunnel. Which one do you fancy?' Plus, 'Are you having problems with that umbrella? I'll ask Tom if he can fix it.' The tube feels safe which walking home or jumping into an Uber doesn't. It's full of people who will come to your aid and it's – and here's the zinger – unbelievably fast. Need to get anywhere in this capital city? Don't even think about driving or a bus. Descend into that secret world and whizz to wherever you want to go. Are you familiar with Harry Potter's portholes? He can get anywhere immediately – well, we have that on our doorstep.

And if I can keep the magic theme going, what's so wonderful about the tube is there is no visible transition. You get on in a busy, cramped part of town. People are rushing to get home, there's hustle and bustle and noise and you descend into the warren. Fifteen minutes later, like a rabbit, you come out into a sleepy, green, completely and utterly different London. It's a dreamlike experience however much you do it and whichever route you take (I love coming up the stairs into mayhem).

What happens when you're down there is important too. It's lovely to be off, to have a bit of time to yourself, to hit shut down. Your phone is defunct and nobody can contact you. You can read a paper, get out a book, have a small daydream or listen to a podcast or some music. Going underground is basically the same as a spa break (OK, maybe not at 8.50am or 5.45pm, but bear with me). You're not pleading with inanimate objects (traffic lights, please turn green, please turn green) or shouting at a new one-way system or screaming inside because 'this bus is being kept at this stop to regulate the service'. You are calm, you are at peace, you have given yourself up to the train and you relinquish all control. Yes, it might be a bit squished and you might not get a seat but you can wallow in the roaring, screeching quiet. You're right, it shouldn't make sense, but it does.

In those special tunnels there is also a lovely unwritten code. I do the same trip every morning with my daughter. We're on our seventh year so you could say we're experts. It's 7.45am and everyone else in the carriage is an aficionado too. We know when we can stand unaided and we're also very aware of the swift turn between Tottenham Court Road and Oxford Circus. The rest of the commuters and school goers are also aware that it gets wobbly and there's a rather beautiful (I'm not exaggerating) chorus of arms that calmly but decisively reach up to grab onto something five seconds before the lurch. We're in a club, we're part of a team, these are our people.

I also love its design. It's a marvel of architecture and engineering. My favourite stations are Marble Arch and Chalk Farm for sentimental reasons, just because they've been my stops, but have you ever been to East Finchley? It's like an art deco palace. Have you considered going to Southwark? It's a present for the eyes and soul and Covent Garden is wholly made up of sunshine yellow tiles. Even if the play, dinner, date was a bit blah you'll skip home, basking in its glow.

The tube is the breathing, living heartbeat part of London – a real reason why this city is the greatest in the world. Rio knocks the wind right out of you with its rugged nature and its people but you will spend at least three hours a day on a bus or in a car. They don't have the magic train so *obrigada*, London and our beautiful tube wins.

FASHION

Fashion is art.

There, boof, I've said it. I was going to spend a couple of sentences, maybe a whole paragraph skirting round the issue, to ease us all in. To try to convince you, if you needed it. But the bottom line is that beautiful fashion stories and ads can blow our minds. Fashion is punchy, it's unapologetic, it's supermodels stalking down the catwalk, it's an image of Cindy Crawford wearing a swimsuit pushing a pram by Herb Ritts that has never really left my brain. It's some of the world's greatest photographers showing us what they can do. It's the Met Ball, it's Kate, it's glossed-back hair, it's the perfect shot, it's sex and it's pure, unadulterated attitude.

There she is, a hat on, knee-high boots and standing by a stairwell. So much thought, so many minds, an array of mood boards would have gone into just that image. There's the lighting, the hair and make-up, the model. Who is the perfect Celine girl, the Versace girl, the Stella girl?

If I want to escape, if I want to daydream, I don't look at photos of George Clooney or Brad Pitt. Other than the odd Google search for sleeping otters (they hold each other's hands so they don't lose each other in the sea, come on) I mainly trawl the fashion sites. They are my Candy Crush, my Words With Friends, my WhatsApp group, my meditation. I rarely add to basket but I love scrolling through them all – Net-a-Porter,

Topshop, Matches, H&M, Katharine Hamnett, it doesn't matter. If there are jeans and shoes to ogle at then I'm in. My Instagram is just a constant feed from designers and fashion editors. Oh look, Gucci has done butterflies; wowzer, Saint Laurent has a new velvet tuxedo. Even though I only really wear one 'look' I still admire them all.

I love the way a fashion campaign can wake us up, style-wise. An arresting fashion image can give us ideas, we can pick and choose which aspect we want to emulate – can't do the miniature satchel but I have old boots in the cupboard from 2010 and I'm going to dust them off. We don't have to immediately go out and buy the bag to be part of it (some cost the same as a two-week holiday in Maui) but we can still pore over the photos. We can still be in awe.

My first proper job was as a fashion assistant. I was in charge of steaming, ordering clothes in, sending them back, helping out on shoots, making the tea and I completely loved it. I was just out of university and marvelled at the sheer bonkers glamour of it all. I went, when I was very lucky, to the odd fashion show and clapped my hands raw when the designer came out at the end to take a bow.

Contrary to some beliefs (thank you *The Devil Wears Prada*), the fashion world is not made up of baddies who are all involved in a conspiracy to convince you to spend £800 on a kaftan before promptly announcing the following year that kaftans are over and out. But editors have pages to fill: the latest creations from many different designers to report on and promote. There are a few longstanding myths in the world of fashion promoted in the pages of those glossy magazines heavy with perfume samples that I feel it would be helpful to draw your attention to and, if possible, dispel once and for all.

WINTER WHITE

You will have noticed these fashion shoots in autumn. In deepest, coldest winter the suggestion seems to be that we throw on a pair of off-white lounge pants, a shiny pale camisole and maybe sit next to an immaculately arranged vase of ivory lilies with a perfect snow scene behind us.

Why not hand round a tray of sticky canapés or mugs of mulled wine in a silky white jumpsuit and pale suede boots? Or do a Sudoku encircled by kids feverishly tearing into Quality Street whilst wearing a pristine bleached dress? Or why not be like our model here? She's standing next to an actual stag on the top of a moor in a white shearling coat.

None of this is realistic and I don't want you to fall down the rabbit hole like I did. In 2003, I had a nine-month-old and a hankering for a white fluffy sweater. I'd seen the ads, I'd bought the bullshit. I thought, I haven't lost a pound since the birth but that's what I'll do, get some sparkling white clothes – I'll feel so good. So Christmassy, so fashion.

You know how this ends but I'll tell you anyhow. It was 23 December and people were coming round. (I can go into pin-sharp details here as even though it was nearly eighteen years ago I remember everything.) I zipped my bulging C-section Shar-Pei stomach into brand new coated white jeans and then rammed a white sweater over my slightly stained maternity bra. I'd put on a whole lot of fake tan the night before and I thought, 'This is it, I'm back. Guys, welcome to our flat, look at the baby, have a drink, we've made food,' (crisps and nuts in bowls was food then). Then, just before the doorbell went, my little puppy of a child was sick all over me (not a dribble). Plus, he'd just eaten curry.

I cried. I never cry over clothes – who gives a toss? Just a top, no bother, I'll brush it off. And you know why? Because they're usually black. The night wasn't ruined (my husband found me tearful in our bathroom and gave me his huge navy sweater) and we all ate Pringles and drank wine. But there's a moral here. Winter white – for fashion shoots only. Not for real life.

THIS SEASON'S SWEATER IS THIN! BUY SIX!

Is there anything on earth less sexy than a base layer? I'm not talking about butter on crumpets (butter is *extremely* sexy), I'm talking about the skin-tight little sweaters that outdoor people wear which have also been chucked down our necks as fashion must-haves. Want to feel cool? Get a transparent jumper.

Now, if you're climbing a mountain then it makes sense – layer up. Wear a paper-thin white polo-neck under a thin fleece top under a pair of rayon dungarees under a skinny thermal winter warmer. You're hiking in the hills and while I wouldn't say I'm happy about your get-up, it is intelligent dressing. It's freezing up there and all you have are some protein bars, a few Day-Glo sticks and a Thermos. Keep warm, keep safe, don't worry about being fashion-forward.

For everyone else back on flat land these ridiculous objects need to stop. Who wants to wear a sweater so thin we can see your bra clasp? Guys, don't do it. Sweaters should be chunky, oversized and preferably cable knit.

THIS IS *SO* NOW

This is the sort of fashion that happens when all the designers get together on Zoom and place a bet. Balaclavas, for example.

'Let's see if they'll buy it!' howls one.

'This is going to be fantastic. We'll put a double G on it!' shouts someone from Gucci, 'there will be a waiting list!'

They all scream and sip negronis and try to come up with the oddest thing imaginable. (See also: clogs, tartan from top to toe, bejewelled crocs and bum bags.)

It goes without saying that balaclavas should be avoided. Don't fall for it. Absolutely OK on Bella Hadid. The rest of us need to wear hats and use scarves to protect our ears. And that's the end of it.

LOGOS

There are acres and acres of fashion pages saying we have to wear clothes with the designer's name on it. Look at this Balenciaga-emblazoned scarf; why not invest in this Fendi swimsuit with Fs all over it? If you've got a massive bank balance and aren't worried about getting bored with something and giving it away six weeks later then fine, yes. Go ahead. For the rest of us unlabelled is the answer. The best dressed rarely wear clothes covered in letters and don't need the 'look at me' status because they're already cool. Mary-Kate and Ashley Olsen should be our fashion heroes. Long black coats, big boots, maybe some mittens. Well done girls.

KITTEN HEELS ARE VITAL

I have an awful lot to say about these horrors so I'm hoping you're sitting comfortably. Let's be frank, of all the animals we should want to be associated with, kittens are at the bottom, right next to the vampire bat and dung beetle, and even then those two would be preferable (the former is vicious but shy and the second doesn't smell great but isn't afraid of hard work). Sure, kittens are cute and fuzzy but also a bit weak. Kittens can't stick up for themselves and if they do want to say something it sounds like a whine. They are cute for around five minutes and then they turn into grumpy, rotund, judgemental cats.

Also, there's that whole *other* kitten connotation, the come-hither kind. The type whose uplifted and separated bosom will ooze out of an overly tight bodice whilst she's reclining on a piano licking a rose stem. A sex kitten. Please somebody pass me a bucket – it's just so uncool, so try hard, so painful, so all-out embarrassing.

I should add at this point, if you have endless, lean, giraffe-like pins then it's true, you can wear anything on your feet. You can even pull off an ankle sock and a sandal and still look great. For the rest of us with normal calves, a kitten heel is an aesthetic disaster. How to shorten and highlight a stocky ankle? Look no further. Throw on a pencil skirt too and all of a sudden, you look two dress sizes bigger. Ten out of ten.

I'm for comfort, such as a sneaker or a brogue, or tremendous ankle pain caused by heels so high you can only walk with help, either in the shape of waist-height furniture or a friend. I don't balk at applying a touch of Deep Heat to a knee at the end of a great night. But the kitten heel is a strange mix of the two – both debilitating and half relaxing. This is confusing. You think you can run for a bus but you look deeply awkward doing it. Avoid.

BUY IT AGAIN!

Fashion will tell us one is not enough. We need a plethora of trousers, we need a mountain of tops. Only one pair of sliders? Don't be silly! They're over here! Buy three for the price of two!

We have new blazers, fashion says. These are different. Come. Come. Look. This one has epaulets. This one is very dark green. Enter our Blazer Land and get a new one. You need a new one.

No, we simply do not. A blazer is one of a number of items that you do not need in all sorts of variations. Perhaps you think you want a blazer with extra-large buttons? If you're a kids' TV presenter and wearing plaits this is fine. You might want a red one; if you present a morning news show then please continue. But most of us muggles just need a great black one. And before you get all, 'Babe, this isn't *Working Girl*, we don't need one at all,' can I just remind you that if you can find a blazer with a very sexy sharp shoulder and mid-length sleeve (not too long, we're not orang-utans) then it will be the best item in your wardrobe. Mine is from Zara, is ten years old and I wear it all the time. Over a dress, with pirate boots, with a slouchy t-shirt and jeans. Anytime you're going out and have to look half decent. So get one, have one. But not more than one.

Here are some items we only need one of:

- Satchel

- Gym shoes

- Big winter coat

- Hoop earrings

- Gold studs

- Straightforward belt

- Dressing gown

- A smart black-tie dress

- Black stilettos

Whenever Fashion Land says you need a surplus of one of the above take a deep breath and remind yourself that you don't.

Fashion shoots and ads are the greatest fantasy that exists. Dive in, drink it all up. When and if we meet I'd like to talk to you about Manolo Blahnik shoes and Louis Vuitton coats. Enjoy the breathtaking images and let them inspire you. But beware of the feeling we have to keep up, that we have to dress in exactly the 'right' way right now. Do some of it but it's a solid no to winter white, balaclavas and please don't even think about kitten heels …

CHARLIE BUCKET AND ELLIOTT

Other than my parents, step-parents, Pink Cat (not a real cat) and my brother and sister, the two most important people in my life growing up were Charlie Bucket and Elliott from *E.T.* Both blew me for six, knocked me sideways, wouldn't quite leave my heart and my head.

At the beginning, I wasn't into books and this must have alarmed my parents. My dad was a publisher, my mum a journalist, my stepmum a copywriter and my stepdad a journalist too. They lived for words – crosswords, puzzles, chatting, what's your favourite word this week, do you think marshmallow is a good one or too long? What would be a good word to describe those clouds? Ah. 'Fluffy' again? OK. That was the car chat. I liked playing shops (till really, really late. Actually, if you gave me a fake till and some plastic pizza right now I'd be happy all day) and never seemed to lose myself in literature.

They'd tried to encourage me, there were weekly trips to the library and small incentives – 'if you get through this Enid Blyton we might have a choc ice at the weekend' – but none of it had made the slightest difference. But then, quite by accident,

I came across a Roald Dahl book and, bored, picked it up.

I read *Charlie and the Chocolate Factory* from start to finish in two days (this was a miracle, I refused to read the back of a cereal packet). I even pretended I was ill so didn't have to go to school. I was mesmerised by the factory, by his grandparents, Violet and of course Willy Wonka but it was Charlie who never exited my brain. What would Charlie do? I'd think that when I was in maths, in P.E., at home with my siblings. He was so good, so thoroughly decent. He passed a test that I know I would have failed. I'd never been so mesmerised by one human being – he was so selfless, always hungry and cold but never complaining, the epitome of an unassuming hero. I'd talk about him all the time. 'But why Mum, why would he give the sweet back?' and 'Would you, Dad? Would you have done?' He was deep-down good but also not wet and this, to a ten-year-old, was almost a miracle. Through Charlie, I wanted to read all of Dahl's works – I inhaled every single one and read *James and the Giant Peach* over eighteen times. You can test me when we meet.

———

The first time I went to the cinema, properly out, was to see *E.T.* It was 1982 and I was ten. I was allowed to bring a friend (Joanna, same class) and it was a seriously big deal. I had a velvet poncho and patent shoes for the trip. Can I just take a moment here to say thanks to my mum as she's allergic to velvet. Not as in 'it's not her favourite fabric' but she'll squeal and jump a mile if she touches it. I'm not sure how you feel about bird-eating tarantulas or heights – yes, that. She once yelped in a shop so loudly when she accidently touched some on the rails we were immediately asked to leave. But she still let me wear this poncho, my favourite piece of clothing (a therapist would have a field day – how much did I want to punish her?).

It was a Saturday night and she bought us tiny paper bags of popcorn beforehand (literally six kernels, the world has changed). We went into the inky black. As we watched, we were transported. We got lost in a screen bigger than we'd ever seen, in the swells of music, in the sheer scale and drama of the story. Here was this young boy who was going to save an alien. He didn't look particularly special, he didn't have a sword (this was a big deal), he wasn't a brainbox, he was, like Charlie, outwardly quite ordinary. But of course he was deep-down kind and well, good.

Three-quarters of the way through my eyes were scratchy and hot. I didn't understand. 'What's happening?' I whispered to my mum. 'Why does the back of my throat hurt? Why am I sad?'

Mum very carefully leant over and, without touching my poncho, explained that the film was making me cry.

Can you imagine? It had never happened to me before. All I'd seen was *Tom and Jerry* and *Playschool* – cartoon animal violence and educational cheer. There hadn't been any *feelings*. Here was boy ready to risk it all for someone he'd just met.

It instantly became my favourite film of all time. Of course I hadn't really seen any other films at this point, but do you know what? It still is. For sentimental reasons, because it was my first film and it affected me so much, because the score alone makes me feel like I'm wrapped in velvet, for E.T. himself and specifically because of Elliott – Elliott was the one.

At university, our Rembrandt tutor (a brilliant man called Jean Michel Massing) let us have a week off Dutch Art and said we could write about anything that moved us. I nervously suggested I could write about the similarities between the two soft yet principled heroes in a kids' book and a Spielberg film. He tutted and said a break from Amsterdam meant a quick 2,000 words on Chagall or Matisse. So I never got to put both their names down on paper at the same time.

Following poor, kind Charlie into that chocolate factory, or seeing Elliott find a friend in E.T. to the sounds of John Williams, really did move me. They showed me another world.

They taught ten-year-old me that you don't have to be outwardly spectacular to be, well, spectacular.

WEDDINGS

I do understand that weddings are some people's idea of hell. There are the screaming toddlers, the standing around on uneven, sodden grass sipping warm wine, the plethora of rock-hard sugared almonds. There are pissed uncles, miniature Yorkshire puddings that are both wet and dry and often an alarming amount of bunting. Let's also mention here the dodgy sound systems, the whispered or shouted speeches (gang, can we use normal voices please), the flesh-coloured tights and usually a dress code.

Some people would prefer jury duty, babysitting a four-week-old with colic or a sexy weekend away with Matt Hancock (OK, maybe I've gone too far here). Well, that, ladies and gents, is not me. I love the receiving line, the posing for photos, the hymns, the weeping mother-in-law, the conga, the flowers, the discussion about the weather, the vicar/rabbi/registrar, the ex who's scowling at the bar and the toasts.

I love the emotional dad and the friends who have never met, the person who decided to go off piste and bring a personalised wooden goat for a present (where shall I put it? Uh, in the bin?) and the overtired bridesmaids. I'll even wear a hat for god's sake, I love weddings that much (this is quite major – I really dislike hats).

I've been to fancy ones and not fancy ones and I can't really tell the difference. At some you will be served organic, artisan walnut bread next to four-tiered Murano glass candelabras; at others there will be a bag of crisps next to a tea light. At one wedding I went to there was a bowl of mini Boursins on all the tables and it was one of the best nights of our lives. We drank, we danced, we all smelt of garlic and woke up the next morning with tiny pieces of foil down our tops. Let's be frank, nobody leaves a wedding and says, 'You know what, that chicken was exceptional.'

The wonderful thing about weddings, when all is said and done, is the extraordinary, the quite frankly ridiculous atmosphere of optimism. They've known each other for six months, cheers to them! He's absolutely on the rebound from the love of his life but let's raise a toast to the happy couple! They don't seem to like each other very much and have argued solidly for the last six years but they've decided to do it anyway. *Masel tov*! I reckon he's already flirting with her friend but here we are in a tent in Cumbria and may they find lifelong happiness! Hip hip hooray.

In the real, normal world we know that relationships should last, you know, just a bit. We realise that if we're incredibly lucky we'll still be talking in five years, maybe eight. With our brains turned on and focused, without all the wedding white noise, we know that the odds are stacked against us – if we glance at statistics we'll see that it's likely he'll be back on Bumble within eighteen months and she can only have sex if she fantasises about the bloke she still loves from college. Marriage is a preposterous proposal. I get bored of sweaters after four years, how on earth can I stay with an actual human for so long? I'll know them too well, they'll be too annoying, they'll wind me up as only they know how. Seriously, how – HOW? – will this ever work? But so far, for me anyway, it has. Nobody is more surprised than I am.

Getting married feels like betting on a donkey in the Grand National, it's like buying a lottery ticket, it's baking a Victoria sponge without a recipe (only one in ten turn out edible – trust me, I've tried). It's like assuming it will be sunny on your one day off, it's like trusting the boiler will work for ever.

Now, of course we cross all our fingers we've chosen someone kind. Someone who will deliver a Lemsip and a Toblerone at 4am, who will say we look amazing when we are wearing jeans two sizes too small and a comedy sweater with a robin on it (I told you I love Christmas), who will carry us to the cab after one too many tequilas and who will rub our back after we gave that 'it looks a bit pink' chicken a go.

We pray we've got a person who is willing us on to tell a funny story and won't look at us flabbergasted from the other side of the table, only to pipe up at the last minute, 'But love, it didn't happen like that, you're exaggerating again.' We can only hope against hope we've opted for someone who won't have a system for filling a dishwasher (guys, give it up – stuff goes in and then it comes out. Yes, I've been known to put a frying pan over the cutlery box but here's the big news, we all survived) and we really hope that we'll actually want to get old with the person we've chosen. But we have to admit, it's a bit bloody nuts.

And yet at weddings any niggles, any worries are thrown out of the window. The joy and happiness in the room is contagious; we cheer when they kiss after their vows and we watch them dance their first jig/waltz/stumble full of adoration and love. And of course there's the dress.

A wedding dress might be my favourite piece of clothing ever. The cumulative gasp as she walks into the church/barn/pub. It doesn't matter if it's lacy, green, puffy, low cut and red or actually shorts and wellies. It's all about that outfit. I think the reason I love them so much is that they're totally secret. If you're close to the bride you might have chosen it with her, might have been there the first time she tried the dress on but if you're one step removed you're all being let into this wonderful first show. She also didn't need approval from him, she might choose something she drew on her school maths book when she was six, she might go with more of a nightie vibe.

The absolute best bit about it is that it doesn't matter. There is no 'perfect' wedding dress. It's her pick, it's her choice and in a world where we ask 'What do you think babe?' we don't with this one. We drink tea or booze with our mum and our mates and just go, 'Yeah, that one.'

I was young when we got married. We didn't have money and I found a lovely dressmaker who made me a dress that resembled an enormous meringue. It was, let's be serious, absolutely disgusting but here's the thing – who cares? We did it (I had to have a nap halfway through, weddings are great but long) and here we are. It doesn't make any sense, but best not to analyse it, eh?

So here's a toast: to bonkers, nonsensical, are-they-out-of-their-minds confidence. Screw statistics and let's raise our glasses to an unfathomable leap of faith. In a world that has to make sense, getting married doesn't make sense at all and that's great.

Quite
TRUE

PARENTHOOD

Let me start this by immediately saying I'm not an expert. In fact, I just told my fourteen-year-old that I was writing a chapter on parenting. It was eight minutes ago and she's still laughing.

If you are planning on being a mum, can I just fill in some gaps that might be missing from your parenting books? Perhaps you have some excellent friends who have already done it and have told you about some of the lesser discussed details. But just in case they haven't, I do think it's good to be aware of certain things, beyond birthing plans, where to get good maternity jeans and the technique of fitting a car seat.

If you don't want to have a baby then I totally get that. Skip this next bit as you'll fall asleep with boredom. But if you do want one, if you can't wait to have a baby and all the biological stars align, then have one. Have lots. Have as many as you can fit into your life, if that's your thing. Don't wait for the perfect moment, don't look at your diary to find just the right time. Don't worry about not being able to drink on New Year's Eve or at your friend's wedding. Don't think, 'But I just got that dress and it's already a bit too tight, I'll take the pill for a bit longer.' If it's even in your head, if it's wafting around your brain, then absolutely have one (they also might take longer to make than you think).

Don't wait for him to turn round and earnestly hand over a book of baby names and a bottle of folic acid. I haven't come across many men who say, 'Yes! Let's completely alter our lives. Who wants to go out drinking and eating and have sex all the time anyway? I'm bored of being number one, I can't wait to be number two! Or in fact, make that number three as your mum will bring round lasagne and that seems more useful and you're super close to your dad so never mind, I'll be last on the list! Let's start now! Are you ovulating?' They don't really do that. They might even say, 'Seriously? But we don't have a spare room.' Your job is to pat them on the head and assure them it'll be fine. It will.

And then you've just given birth. Yes, you're in love. You've never felt anything like it. You thought you loved him, your mum and dad, your siblings, your best friend and you were very keen on that dog for twelve years. There was a time when your heart exploded every time you saw Leonardo di Caprio on screen (early Leo obviously) and once, while drunk, you proposed to a Magnum (double caramel – goes without saying) but *this* love … Well, this is something else.

The eyebrows, the small hands, the neck, the mouth – look at his nose, I've never seen such a nose. You can't stop kissing their ears, their tummies, their ankles. You're overwhelmed and blown away. The hormones kick in and you might cry a bit (or a lot) and you might find certain small tasks like finding cotton wool or washing a bib so overwhelmingly gargantuan that you have to just sit on the floor with your head in your hands. Hopefully you'll have a helpful and kind partner or maybe you'll have a brilliant set of parents and with any luck you'll have great friends who can help or at least be at the end of the phone.

Fine. But I also have to share the other news; the bit that's missing from the new baby blog. Basically, you'll give birth and then, to be honest, your arse is bleeding. Your nipples are angry (don't worry, they don't get left out, they'll bleed too) and your vagina is absolutely livid. You're physically crushed and when you turn over in bed your stomach follows some time later. Your feet grow outwards and get slightly hairy – you've seen a hobbit's foot, right? You won't mind any of this – or, to be more specific, you won't notice any of this. You're so sleep-deprived that you spend much of your time staring into space, when not gazing at the new perfect little bundle. You can't imagine ever leaving the house again in a normal fashion (it took you two hours to get his/her parasol, blanket, hat, spare nappy, bottle, little teddy, two muslins together last week, so you've sort of given up and anyway, the park will wait) so the odd hairy tuft on your foot is the least of your problems.

Then they're suddenly six months old and drinking milk happily and it's under control. They're taking from your boob or a bottle and they giggle and they can sit up and wave their arms. You're so madly in love you can't believe it. You feel sorry for people who don't have your particular baby (this is a hideous trait but don't panic, it doesn't last long). Everything is fine, you feel pretty much back to normal and you're coping.

Then eating the real food starts – easy, right? Except you become so completely obsessed with the 'right' food that you're actually insufferable to be around. Not chicken again, he had it yesterday. I'm thinking of making a fish pie, please go out and get an organic potato, nothing else will do. Thanks for the pear, Dad, did you pluck it from the tree yourself? Are you absolutely certain it wasn't sprayed? Did it come easily away from the stalk? I'm going to steam it now, just need to sterilise everything, can you watch the baby? I'm teaching him what a frog says – we're going with croak rather than 'ribbit', please follow suit. We worry and panic they're getting enough vitamins and then the pear is bruised and you burn the fish pie. You find a slightly less stressful alternative. I still remember the moment I discovered he liked toast. 'Look,' I said. 'Toast and marmite. I reckon we're sorted.'

When you're not steaming butternut squash or wiping down the highchair, floor, ceiling (genuinely, how do they do that?) you will also notice the poo changes. From being silky and milky and mousse-like and practically edible this child is now excreting human faeces. I warned you.

Then this little person learns to walk and potter about but still you follow and kiss and cuddle and smell their ears and knees and elbows (the elbows are really quite something) and play a lot of pat-a-cake.

They get bigger and then they start nursery. You keep everything light and dandy at the school gates while your small, no, make that tiny, perfect human wanders in and learns how to read and write. You pick them up and envelop them into your arms and tell them they're brilliant for trying to hold a pencil and you skip home with their little hand sweetly holding yours.

They spend a couple of years learning songs and playing with sand and miniature teapots and then all of a sudden they bring work home. Homework? What? Learning to read? What's a phonic? Help me someone. It steps up a notch and now we're having to help them with maths. Dividing using the bus-stop method? What the hell is that? Dude, I use this thing called a calculator on my phone.

Don't fear. You can get round all of it by saying, 'Just listen to the teacher baby, I don't want to teach you the wrong way to do things.' It's quite important our kids don't find out how stupid we parents are so you rely heavily on, 'Why don't you just try it yourself and then see what they say at school?'

And then the questions start and they genuinely don't stop. Why is the sky blue? Why do sharks never stop swimming? Why is a scorpion an arachnid? Why do snakes sleep in trees? Why are there different kinds of beans and where do they grow? What is a blood orange? Why do we need to stand in this queue? What is Tampax? How did you make me?

This stage lasts about ten years. If you're patient and friendly and have had a good day then you'll enjoy this. You'll reply with a 'Let's find out!' and will chuck open a search engine and get to the bottom of where, in fact, rainbows do end and what is the difference between an amphibian and a reptile. But if you're me you'll occasionally want to turn round and say, 'No idea mate, to be honest, I need to have a bath.'

They get bigger but they're still seriously cuddly, like small bears. Their friends come over for endless playdates and tumbling and even though Harry or Mary is at your house you're still allowed to give your fuzzy offspring a hug. They're older, bigger, they've learnt how to do up their shoes and cut their own sausages but still, there are major kisses on the neck and arms wrapped round their small bodies. As they're watching *Finding Nemo* on a Sunday afternoon, lost in the world of clownfish and octopi, it's totally OK to give them a back scratch or tickle their toes. They might brush you off sometimes but they'll always come back to sit on your lap for reading a story or a good conversation about the extraordinary power of dinosaurs or ketchup.

Then they're twelve, maybe thirteen, and you kiss them goodnight and tell them to have sweet dreams and they cosily wander up to bed. You might follow them up for a last snuggle and you'll help them organise their toys or their pillow and you'll watch them brush their teeth and you'll tell them to make sure the bed bugs don't bite and you pull their door just to and blow them a kiss. This is wonderful you say to yourself, they are wonderful and nothing will ever change.

The next morning, with absolutely no warning whatsoever, your beloved child, the only person who you want to squeeze all day and all night, wanders into the kitchen and has turned (dramatic music please) into a teenager.

Here's the bad news – the touching has gone. Whoosh, disappeared. You can't rub their backs or stroke their eyebrows; a kiss before bed is almost banned and dropping them at the school gates (even from afar) is 'mortifying'. They're independent, not interested in being given a peck on the cheek, they talk about space. Parents are clingy, embarrassing and overly affectionate.

In this new, cold world you become ever more desperate. You're leaving out small bits of Lego so they stand on it and hurt their foot so will let you cuddle them better. They realise this is happening and learn to dance across the floor like contortionists to avoid the accidents. You're waiting for them to get a cold so you can take their temperature and then they (might) accept a hug.

They bat you off, they don't want to talk about what happened in geography or if they're still best friends with so-and-so. They have phones now and you're merely a feeder, a cab driver and someone with a wallet. You try to find out what they're into – 'Shall we watch *Stranger Things* together?' 'Do you fancy a trip to Yo Sushi? Topshop?' But all is met with aloofness and pity. You are the dullest person on earth. You are an embarrassment.

And this is possibly the most important role of all. Whatever happens, your kids have to find you completely agonising. You can try to keep up with their music tastes (dancing to Billie Eilish at 48, let's not do that) and you can ask to watch or take part in their TikToks (again, this is not for you). You can pull up a bean bag when they have friends round and say 'What's the news?' but please know that your main role, the whole reason you're there (because they've learnt how to make sandwiches and pasta at this point), is to embarrass them. They find you cumbersome, ancient, thick, annoying and mainly they don't want you near their friends.

When the sleepover is over, when the FaceTime has ended, then maybe you can have a miniature chat, but if there is any audience at all (I'm not just talking about the opposite sex here) then know, in their eyes, you're a total muppet. Because of this you won't be able to help yourself but you will actually be even more embarrassing than you're supposed to be. It's a self-fulfilling prophecy.

When my son was fourteen I took him to school on the tube and we bumped into a pack of 'cool kids' from his class and I started trying to breakdance (I have never done this before in my entire life). It was chronic, it was mortifying for him and terrible for them. I was bang on I reckon. Because here's the thing – you're supposed to be an awful, humiliating person. Don't try and keep up with them, be permanently befuzzled. That's your job.

Alongside embarrassing them, your other duties include annoying them and hassling them. You ask about homework, you ask them several times to put a wash on/empty the dishwasher/grab the such-and-such from upstairs on the thingy but they want to go to the Co-op with their friends so they'll need some money. They won't want to cuddle you or chat to you and they'll roll their eyes every time you suggest a family activity, but they do need some dough. They won't try and cover it up. They'll just expect it. Make them get a job the second they're sixteen. Not so they spill coffee on unsuspecting clientele but because then they'll understand that £10 is £10.

But even this stage cannot last for ever. I am not at this point yet with my kids (I can't wait), but I do remember the moment I realised my parents were actually clever. I thought they were annoying with their cuddles and their endless chat and questions. I couldn't imagine they had anything to teach me and then, boom, one summer when I was eighteen, I worked out I should maybe listen to them. Wait just a second, they're actually quite smart. They'd been there and done that.

An example. My dad told me not to fill the gaps in conversation when talking to work about a raise. I was working in a cafe and they expected us to do extra hours for no more pay. He advised me to ask for what was fair and then not speak. It sounds so simple but it doesn't come naturally. There's a gap in conversation, there's a pause – don't worry, I'm a young woman and I'll fill it! Nope, don't. Just sit, just wait, just don't make everything all right, zip your mouth up tight. Then good things happen.

My mum told me quite seriously to be the first at work and always be the last. 'But Mum, I'm just waitressing, I'd done eight hours, they said I could go.'

'No baby, stay and be friendly. You'll become indispensable.'

At this stage I was working at Maria's Coffee Lounge, I was still young but she had a good point. I could always catch an extra shift when I wanted one, which was excellent if I wanted a new top or a noodle takeaway.

———

Then one day – and I know this is coming – they leave. Gone. Bye. Thanks, and all that. You've worshipped them, cooked for them, educated them and watched from the sidelines as they've been happy, sad, worried, rebellious, kind, selfish. You've tried to create the best creatures possible – secure, selfless, confident, humble, funny – and then those puffins are out of the door. Is that you calling again? But we spoke yesterday. Sure, we might come at the weekend but we might also stay in bed.

You constantly watch videos of when they were little and, when they eventually return your calls, you start every sentence with, 'Do you remember that day in Wales when we fed a baby lamb?' and 'Can you believe we gave you a tortoise for your seventh birthday? You were so happy!' and 'Whatever happened to that friend who moved to Glasgow?' and they do their best to appease. They nod and say, 'I remember,' even if they don't.

There's very little point to us, anymore. Sure, they love us but we're, well, parents. We're old, we're the same, we're solid.

But I have good news. I think I'm miles away from this point, but just based on my own experience at the other end I give you this. One day, out of nowhere, they really need us again. Because your child has a baby and suddenly it's your turn to make the lasagne or pick the pear that hasn't been sprayed. We're immediately useful, we buy cots and nappies and have all the time in the world to hear about how he said 'dada' and why he prefers mango to apple. They come back to us and now they've made magical unicorns that you love just as much as them. To my kids then, no rush but I'm right here with your old books and teddies, I am a 24/7 babysitting service and I can't bloody wait.

So there you are - the potholes and the great in a small chapter. You need to know two things; your body eventually recovers (your feet become feet again) and yes, my daughter is still laughing.

SQUIRREL ETIQUETTE

Look, I don't know how to say this but my eight-year-old son is quite insistent that this be added to the book.

He asked me what I was writing about and I told him but he was completely unimpressed. I asked him what he thought I should add. Here it is.

'Mum, I'd like you to write about how to behave around squirrels in the park.'

'Um, are you serious, Bear?'

'Yes. There should be rules and I don't think anyone has published the rules of squirrel etiquette.' After some discussion and a few edits, here we go.

1. If you spot a squirrel then you are allowed, in fact encouraged, to walk up to him/her making a little kiss noise so that he knows you're there (it's more of a click click sound).

2. If he is not too scared (scaring a squirrel is an absolute no no) then offering an unsalted nut (preferably of the monkey variety, we've looked into it) is absolutely fine.

3. If the squirrel is a little jumpy or nervous then the human must move on. Leave a nut in view but please don't throw it at the jazz rat (sorry, fluffy animal).

4. If someone else has also spotted the squirrel then you need to, through eye contact and possibly a small bow or nod of the head, work out who will be approaching.

5. If this person has a child with them younger than yours that immediately means they get the first feed. Stepping back at this point is the right thing to do. Watching from afar is totally fine. Please do not hold out a nut at this point. This can be confusing for all parties.

6. If someone is bending down and already connecting (his word, not mine) with a squirrel then this animal is absolutely out of bounds. Don't approach, don't make the squirrel noise and let them have their moment. This is very important.

7. If there is a cluster of squirrels you cannot 'take' them all. Don't be greedy and although being kind and generous with nuts is good, another family might be right behind you and you don't want them to be too full up.

8. Saying that, if there's nobody about and it's started to drizzle let them feast.

9. If there is a squirrel and pigeon cluster then be aware the birds might get a little over-excited and start pecking the squirrels. Please make sure you aim the nut close to the squirrel and as far from the birds as possible. (I don't want to get too specific here but a pigeon will depart if an arm is lifted with some force. Scares a bird, not a rodent. This has been tried and tested.)

10. Finally, enjoy your squirrel time and please never make fun of them. Don't call them rodents (they don't like it) or heavy-set or aggressive. They are proud mammals and desire your respect.

YOU MUST STAY WITH HIM IF

We've seen the very serious warning signs that mean you should run a mile from a man. Waiting 30 minutes in the rain for a cab? Watching him apply two different moisturisers before bed? You're alright mate. Bye. But the reasons someone turns out to be a keeper can be as strange and as vital, too.

HE LAUGHS AT YOUR JOKE MORE THAN ONCE

There are six of us having dinner. My friend is hilarious; she's building up to a great story and we can all feel it. Something happened a couple of weeks ago at work; she's laughing as she gets to the good bit. We're drinking beer, we're full of jalfrezi and there's a sparkle in her eyes. She's brilliant at accents, she's excellent at putting us all right there, bang in the middle of the story, she's a master at building tension. We're all completely enthralled as she delivers a killer punchline, we're howling, some of us are banging the table and I'm actually clapping. This is laughter and friendship and why going out (even when we're knackered) is great. It's like a tonic, it makes up for the packed tube, the office politics, the endless chats with an aunt about whether hand towels should be square or rectangular. As the hilarity dies down I look over at my friend's husband and he is simply basking in her brilliance.

He's laughing too, he's mesmerised by her ability to make everyone fall about giggling. And here's the thing: he's heard this story at least six times in the last fourteen days. When she first told him, when she was on the phone to her mum, when her brother and his wife came over two nights ago. He doesn't mind, he's not going to cut in with a 'Here we go' or a 'Babe, get to the ending? More wine anyone?' and he just delights in everyone's joy and wonder.

That – right there – is what you want: someone who doesn't steal your thunder, who wants everyone to think 'lucky him' rather than 'lucky her'. And that makes you both lucky. If he gets crotchety when the spotlight is on you, if he starts to comment on something else when you're in the middle of a joke then he's a bit of a tool. Or just insecure. But neither is going to work. Stay with the boy who always thinks you're the greatest in the room, as that will last.

HE LOVES HIS MOTHER

Not too much, not more than he loves you, but a lot, a real lot. I mean, you don't want to go on every holiday with her, you don't want her to move in. Nothing is less sexy than, 'I like your meatballs but my mum makes them with slightly more sauce, I think she uses paprika, do you think you could ask her for the recipe? Sorry to be a pain.' Of course I could, but then you should know I'm going to start sleeping with someone else so, you know, up to you.

But he has to love his mum. If he loves his then he'll love yours (I can't tell you how important this is) and he'll respect and love women. Beware the man who complains about her calling or wanting to see him. What happened there? That's a string you're going to need to pull on and it might be unpleasant.

HE NEVER USES EXCLAMATION MARKS

'Can't wait to see you!!' Other than opening a message saying 'Do you mind if I bring my friend along so he can watch us have sex?' is there anything worse?

No man or woman should be using !! if they're older than twelve. Being excited does not mean you have to be excited!!! He can be thrilled about seeing you, and you don't want him to be aloof and cool, but an over-enthusiastic user of that particular punctuation point is physically repellent.

You don't want to go out with someone who uses emojis either. You can, your mates can, but if he thinks about texting a cat with heart eyes then I'm afraid it's time to put the flat on the market and look for a divorce lawyer. If I'd wanted to marry a boy, a child, a springy lamb I'd have gone for that nineteen-year-old when I was 32. He's a grown-up and should behave like one.

I just want to add I'm happy if he's keen on full stops. There's something very cool about a full stop. It's the king of points.

HE'S KIND TO THE PERSON WHO TAKES HIS ORDER

Do you know why I married my husband? Well, I was 26, desperate for a baby and couldn't afford to leave home and I liked his flat and he cooked a bloody good burger and also made my head shoot off my shoulders when we took our clothes off. Which are some of the reasons.

He also knows a lot, which is always hot. 'Explain what happened in Suez again?' is my kind of foreplay. I don't need a champagne cocktail, a fancy dinner with three forks or a 'You look stunning' but rather an encyclopaedic knowledge of oak trees, an explanation of why we drive on the left and what exactly happened in 1917 in Russia. I'll tell you what, you keep talking about the history of temples in Kyoto and I'll take my bra off for you.

But other than these little nuggets, what did it for me is how he behaved in restaurants, bars, planes – indeed, simply around people. Thanks so much, no rush, I'll carry it over for you, you look rushed off your feet so we don't need to order now, come back to us at the end, here, have a drink on us. Having been a waitress every school holiday from the age of sixteen, it was just the magic characteristic that tipped me over. I'd been on dates with boys who were slightly entitled – they didn't exactly click their fingers but I could just tell they believed themselves to be better than the person who was putting away their coat, pouring the wine or bringing them a sandwich.

I married him because he always asks his cab driver how his day was; I love the fact he'll never take a seat on the tube; I'm happy he believes in big tips and not making a mess. Obviously don't tell him I've said anything nice about him – most of the time I can be found tutting, eye-rolling and asking him why he chose to put the tuna in the cupboard that's clearly only for rice and pasta. I mean, what is he? An idiot?

HE PROPERLY TALKS TO YOU

Some men go through life adoring their wife and kids but they never really have a conversation. Not a proper one. Not one where they ask how their partner actually is and listen to the answer. They make roasts and book holidays and see friends and everything is surface-fine. But actual, real communication is imperative.

My happiest friends are with men who want to get to the

nub, want to understand. It doesn't have to be 24/7 and nobody wants to be married to someone who endlessly asks for 'catch-up time' (please just make me a bagel and pass the remote, I'm too tired to speak) but they must be able to talk when needed. Not about what time Sainsbury's shuts on a Sunday, not about the mortgage, but genuine conversation. What are you thinking? Did that make you feel weird? Is the sex a bit dull? Talk to me. I've been wondering about how you're taking that news. He needs to be interested and that will make him, rather miraculously, interesting.

HE LAUGHS AT HIMSELF

'What's so funny about my jacket? I bought it in the airport and I think it's great. Yes, that tartan pattern *is* only visible in the sun. What? If you don't like it just say so (pouts).'

Women laugh at themselves all the time – I'm a moron, the soup was both burnt and cold, what am I like? I'm such a clumsy thing, sorry about that wine glass. God, the kids are thick, why hasn't any of it gone in? But some men don't. Find one that does and if he says he's a bit of a loser then, chances are, he probably isn't. A man who takes himself very seriously is unpalatable.

HE RUNS YOU A BATH

This is small, it feels inconsequential, but as we all know there are two ways to run a bath. Shouting 'I've turned on the taps, over to you babe!' while he wanders off to watch the news as you're putting the baby to bed is one way of doing it. The other is, quite frankly, majestic. He gets the temperature right, he adds Badedas, he gets it good and deep and then dims the bathroom light. 'Sweetheart, you sounded whacked earlier. Jump in.

I'll defrost the chicken,' is entirely sexy. This man is deep-down kind. He might do other things that drive you mad but he's altogether good. A keeper.

HE MAKES DINNER WITH APLOMB

Just as with bath running, there are also a couple of ways people can make a meal. One involves using every pot and pan, turning the kitchen upside down, complaining there's no tartare sauce and managing to set the smoke alarm off. This is not relaxing. Then there is the man who happens to cook a lot and not mention it, not constantly fish for compliments or recognition of his extraordinary achievement of heating food and putting it on a plate. Now that's lovely. Also, while we're here, why is it so often the woman's job to cook? There's a subtle but important difference in 'What's for dinner?' and 'What shall we have for dinner?' If you've found one who only says the latter, move in immediately.

HE ASKS US WHAT WE'D LIKE AND LISTENS

About five years ago, I was working too much. Our youngest was three and still slept actually on my neck in our bed – I was so tired I practically walked into walls. Christmas was coming up and he sat me down and said, 'What can I get you?' I had a proper think about this (I usually, of course, say nothing or cheese) and said that I'd like him to take me to the nearby Marriott hotel.

I said, 'Just take me at 3 or whenever I'm allowed into the room and take my phone and leave me there. I want a small room, the smallest there is. I'd like to lie down on the bed, I'd like to order room service, maybe a sandwich and some tea. I'd like to be alone, all alone. I don't want to watch a screen, I don't want to talk to anyone, I just need sixteen hours of sleep and a bath robe that isn't stained.' I thought it was quite dramatic, a real plea, a proper 'help me'. It's genuinely all I wanted at the time.

He listened intently, was quiet and then cracked a huge smile. 'You're hilarious. Don't be nuts. A new black sweater it is.'

He got up from the table and wandered off. But then, rather magically, he doubled back. He swiftly put me in bed, confiscated my phone and took the kids out for a full day and they all slept at my mum's. I gave up some of my work, the small one eventually got used to his bed and I still got a sweater. If you manage to meet someone who really listens and follows through then that's good.

HE'S NOTICED WHAT PERFUME YOU WEAR

Sounds simple, right? I'd like you to call him or ask him right now. Don't give him clues, don't tell him the first letter. Just a simple question. Don't be surprised when he doesn't know. 'Ah, is it in a bottle?' is simply not enough. If you've been together for a long time you'll have garnered a lot of information – you know his nieces' and nephews' birthdays, who his favourite teacher at school was, what vegetable he thinks it is imperative to have with salmon. If he doesn't know what smell you wear then it's a bit disappointing. Men, find out, file it in your brain and sometimes get us some. That's entirely pleasing.

IF HE DOESN'T THINK ONLY YOU DO THE KIDS

Some men assume you're in charge of what afterschool clubs the kids do, whose house they're going to for a playdate on Friday, what present to take to their friend's football birthday party. Because you popped them out, you are somehow responsible for the admin. I know it's slightly more complicated if one of you works full-time and the other doesn't, but it's the *presumption* that gets me. Guys, welcome to the twenty-first century. We both made them, let's continue to work together here. If you're with someone who gets involved, if they open the school emails, if they have a chat with the small person about whether they'd prefer to learn piano or the drums (please let it be the former) then I'm certainly not saying they deserve a medal, but it's still a very good sign.

HE UNDERSTANDS THAT YOUR GIRLFRIENDS ARE SACROSANCT

He gets that you are to be shared. He doesn't ask you to get off the phone with a 'Didn't you two talk this morning?' and he fully grasps the fact that your girlfriends are family, they are sisters, they are the special element that keeps you going, makes you happy and are of vital importance. If your friend starts going out with someone and they disappear, always busy with his friends, this is concerning. It can be a sign that he expects her to fit into his world, that he has little interest in hers. If you find someone who likes, even loves your friends and what you all do for each other this is a sign he's secure, he's happy for you, he wants you to be entirely satiated. Excellent.

POWER

I'm not talking about shoulder pads here. I'm not talking about how many YouTube subscribers somebody has. This is not the time to talk about whether you can get a table at Nobu without a reservation. All of those are indications of clout, sure, but I'd like to talk about a different kind of strength, a special kind of muscle, the kind that will simply floor you.

I don't know how far you live from the National Gallery in London and I don't know if galleries are your thing. I've bored you rigid about Titian but I couldn't possibly publish a book (and they definitely won't ask me to do it again) without mentioning Caravaggio. Yes, the 'bad boy' of art – he died young, was arrested for throwing a plate in someone's face (the argument was about artichokes) and eventually mortally stabbed someone. He paints with ferocity, with guts, with pure, unadulterated power.

If you ever find yourself near the National Gallery in Trafalgar Square, can I tempt you to bolt in and make your way to room 32 to have a gawp at *The Supper at Emmaus*? Now, it's a big room and it's rammed with beautiful works but do me a favour – just zone in on this one. Imagine you're at the best pick 'n' mix in the world but I just want you to go for the fizzy colas. Feels ridiculous but actually rather brilliant and relaxing to focus on only one offering. It was painted in 1601 and is quite simply, extraordinary. It's an early work so still has colour (his painting became almost black and white as he developed) and it is so arresting, so moving, so powerful.

An incognito resurrected Christ is sitting down and eating and Caravaggio paints the exact moment he reveals himself to two of his disciples. Do you feel like you're there? I feel it too. His stillness, his calm, his humanity is thrown into stark relief compared to his two followers. One of them is practically coming out of the work, his arm outstretched to us. This is further magnified as the inn-keeper is still in the dark (in every way). If you just stand in front of it and take it in this image will never leave you. It's a snapshot, it's not of a mood but of a split second, beautifully captured in oils.

We look for power in all sorts of ways – we want our partner to be more forthright, we want our kids to have more gumption and we are attracted (even if we don't like ourselves for it) to people who control the room, the magnets with the authority. But sometimes we need to be reminded of power of a different kind.

We need to be arrested (not actual handcuffs) but stopped in our tracks and this painting will do this with one punch to the gut. There are moments that stay with us, that seem to change the future, however subtly – her blowing out her birthday candles, that fantastic night you both worked out it was better if you did it *that* way, the time your boss turned around and said she thought you had a great future. They're tiny little punctuation marks that stick out and it's extraordinary that this artist, this one man, could capture a single second in such a way. And that, is power.

NURSES

I have been lucky – let's be honest, incredibly lucky – and of that I have no doubt. However, there have been moments in my life (I think there have been those moments in all our lives) – the most terrifying, the most confusing, the most discombobulating – that have led me to believe that the greatest people who walk the earth are nurses.

They are kind, they are clever, they work incredibly hard, they are there to save us, or to help us through it when saving is simply not possible.

They do twelve-hour shifts, they change the bed pans, insert the cannulas, the feeding tube and the drip. They take our temperature, measure our blood pressure and write down the vitals in a special book.

They are the cool, calm voice in the corner of the room. They know when to leave families alone and they know when they are needed. They have a magical sixth sense and will enter and leave a room at exactly the right time. In a fog of panic and worry they are the steady hand, the comforting touch. They arrive at work after a long commute (ask any nurse who works in a large city, none of them can afford to live close to the hospital) and they put on their uniform and are ready to help people who are going through something so raw, so serious and so important.

They hold your hand when your child is going in for an operation, they hold your hand when the surgeon says there's bad news, they hold your hand when the doctor says the medication isn't working.

They clean down the bed after an accident and don't comment, they will help you out of bed when a shower is the best thing for you. They'll bring in an audiobook CD if they think it'll help the pain and they're happy to listen to the same trauma, the same how did this happen over and over and over again. They'll wait an extra half an hour at the end of the day so they can see your test results, they'll make you laugh when it's time for the foul-tasting medicine, they'll sing 'Let It Go' during the barrage of injections and they'll feel uncomfortable when you offer thanks.

They'll tell you that it'll be OK when you know deep down it won't and they'll clear up your sick when you can't make it to the bathroom. They'll hang fairy lights when your daughter asks for them and they'll bring tuna sandwiches from the canteen at odd times of day. They'll get fresh water for a vase and they'll quell the rising panic. They'll walk to the operating theatre and will name the special anaesthetic helping teddy and they'll make sure they tell you when she wakes up. They'll be by your side and they'll make everything better.

They see you at your most vulnerable and are simply there to help. They have so many people to look after on the ward but you know they'll always come back. They place the emergency button in your hand and they say it doesn't matter how many times you press it. They'll explain what morphine does and why she might shout and fight and they'll cut the cake when your hands are shaking too much at the end of the day. They'll make up your bed and say it could be worse, they'll read her a story when you have to make a call.

They'll pick you up and put you and your family back together again.

They are our *Mona Lisa*, they are our everything.

T-SHIRTS

A t-shirt's just a t-shirt, right? It's same old, same old. Wear under a sweater, wear under a jacket, throw it on in the morning, sleep in it or strip it off at night. Big one, little one, old one, soft one. Just pull it over your head, let's not make a huge thing about it. I mean, a burger is a burger. A flat is a flat. A margarita is a margarita.

Woah there. Let's just stop and have a think about this. When you're ten, correct, a t-shirt is just a t-shirt, but when you're as old as me this is very much not the case. In fact, this is a matter of priorities. The stuff we wear all the time is where we need to focus. These are the items that deserve our love and attention. The black-tie event, the fancy dinner – please let's worry about those outfits less. Don't save up and splurge on a bejewelled blazer you're going to wear once a year – instead, let's spend our time throwing our whole hearts into, yes, finding the perfect t-shirt.

A great t-shirt and pair of jeans is genuinely the answer to a fantastic weekend. You're battling with the self-service till at Tesco – I just want two lemons and some gum, why have I set off the alarm and need assistance again? Or, 'Mum, I know it's Sunday but I totally forgot I have to make a Tudor street scene using only pasta. Shall we start now?' Both of these situations are made better if you're in a butter-soft, great fitting t-shirt. We can tackle anything if we're comfy. Silly me, I have worked out the till, please ignore my stupidity. Course we can baby, pass me the penne.

Firstly, the length has to be perfect. Too short and it's nerve-wracking moving too much. Need that tin of tuna on the top shelf? I'm terribly sorry but I simply can't get it. That would mean lifting my arm up as far as it can go and I've got tufts, an acre of stretch marks and, as of late, my stomach skin seems to be made entirely of tissue paper. If I get the tuna all of this will be on show and, I promise, once seen you can't un-see it. Do you remember Jabba the Hutt? Precisely.

Too long and wow, you've got short legs! Or worse, something to hide. Trying to cover your bum? Worried about your lack of belt? Wanna look like E.T.? Why are you dressed like a teenage skater boy? You seem to be on the verge of tying a sweatshirt round your waist and we can no longer do that as we're grown-ups. (And on the subject of grown-ups, anything asymmetric smacks of a midlife crisis or a terrible washing machine shrinking error. A handkerchief hem is only fine if you're pregnant. If you're not growing a human life inside you then your t-shirt has to be the same length all the way round.)

It also has to be soft. In the 90s, scratchy was fine. Hey, this mint green super-coarse jumper is fake mohair but it's cool so I'm going to wear it for twelve months straight until I have a rash over most of my body. But who cares? Darren from round the corner likes it and that's just more important right now. We wore tickly and lumpy fabric for years without realising that there were other options. We were more interested in the colour (I'm going to throw in the memory of tie dye here) and in the (dear god) slogan on the front. Can I just confirm that wearing clothing bearing the words 'daddy's princess' or 'I believe in unicorns' stops at thirteen. This is non-negotiable.

The perfect t-shirt then is made out of something called modal (no idea either but trust me, softer than a kitten's stomach) and it's navy or black or grey (or white, if you're happy with your abdominal muscles and bra choice) and it has either a snug round neck or a loose V (never a square or boat neck — that's an actual order). Please nothing with miniature buttons.

Has everyone followed that? Are we all in agreement? So now that's out of the way, while we're here, maybe a flat is just a flat but we all know a margarita is not just a margarita and a burger is never just a burger. It has to be, respectively, on the rocks with salt, extra lime juice and it has to be from Five Guys. The End.

FAMOUS
PEOPLE

Who are your dream dinner party guests? Ever played that game? I love playing that game, that's easy. I'll take the one who was Doctor Who, the supermodel, that very famous reality star, the lead singer of that band, the ex-president, of course those two sell-out comedians. We'd have moussaka, I'd bake my special sponge pudding and it would be excellent. They're just normal aren't they? They're just like you and me. No. Most probably, A* famous people are absolute turds.

I should say there are different tiers of fame. There are people who are always in the papers, there are soap stars and reality kings and queens who we all feel like we know, there are national treasures whom we all adore. The lower rung might include people who sometimes pop up on telly a few weeks of the year and occasionally get mistaken for Davina McCall in Waterstones (don't worry, I always sign 'Love, Davina'). What I'm talking about here is the very top level, the very peak of international celebrity. And they are, sometimes, absolutely awful.

But the fact is, it's not really their fault. There's a lot of noise around them, a lot of fussing, a lot of worrying and, let's be frank here, an awful lot of panic.

At the beginning, before they became fully fledged stars, they were probably embarrassed when asked what they'd like. 'Please, I don't need a rider. Come on, I just sing songs/act. I'll make my own way there.' But after they were asked a few more times, perhaps seen what others have in *their* dressing rooms, it became slightly more: 'Well, if you're really asking I do like Itsu and I prefer a BMW to an Addison Lee. Thanks so much.' And then that quickly escalated and soon the list of requirements covers four pages of A4.

They become stratospheric and it's first class to crazy town. Suddenly they have an army of people whose job it is to cater to their every imagined, perceived, totally invented whim. Having once said they'd be happy with Pringles the make of the water is now listed and a seaweed salad (recipe included) has to be made by a celebrated chef. Cutlery is asked for, nothing used before, please.

'This room is ever so slightly too cold, who has a thermometer? Can we get some blankets in here? Not merino, arsehole, I'll need cashmere. Navy or cream, never black, and she hates green wool. Of course three ply. Jesus. She takes her tea slightly darker, please get that out of here because if she sees it there'll be hell to pay.

'Um, I don't think you quite understand, we asked for peonies and not roses, was the email not clear? Maybe I spelt it wrong? No, I don't think so either. Where are these from? Esso? This room will never do, please take us to a larger one and he's absolutely going to need more towels. And a wooden floor will work better than carpet, surely someone can fix this overnight? One more thing, we requested a Diptique candle; this one is called Winter Spice and it's from somewhere called The White Company? And there seems to be a sticker on it that says 'Thank you for coming to Bicester'. Don't make me cancel this booking.

'She's going to need the mango in thinner crescent shapes, use a ruler to measure if you need to, these appear to be cut into hefty chunks. I don't know if you've ever dealt with a lump of mango whilst wearing lip gloss? Thought not, it's an absolute mess, a disaster, a car crash of stickiness. This is not a fruit plate, this looks like a bowl for a kids smoothie-making session. Remove at once and while you're there I'd like a matcha latte, extra hot, medium cup, one stevia sachet and a biodegradable stirrer. Oh, and are you going to be wearing those dungarees when she gets here? She likes people around her not to look like children's entertainers, put on a suit.

'Why is this picture up over here? This is one of his biggest competitors. We're going to need to take it off the wall. I don't care that he did six sold-out nights here last spring, it really will put our artist in a terrible mood, it needs to be replaced and dear god, is that a *yucca*? We specifically said palms.'

And this is all before the star has arrived, before they've even walked in the room. The scene has to be perfect, nothing is out of place, the lighting is just so, the melon has been carved into the shape of a swan. The phone calls, the progress reports are minute-by-minute. 'She's coming.' 'Five minutes ETA.' 'Please be ready.' 'She's going to need something to eat – an avocado wrap, hold the avocado?' And the worst: 'I see. She slept badly.'

'People, let's get ready, everyone at their stations, be bright, be upbeat. Louis, that joke you told at supper in Paris two weeks ago that made her almost laugh? Use it. Seriously, everyone eyes forward, we'll get through this. Let's not mention it's number five in the charts. If she asks, we haven't been told by the official iTunes people where it's placed yet. Just change the subject. Sam, remember to ask to see a picture of the kids, say something about their teeth, she just had them whitened. It's a go everyone, we have 60 seconds. She's in a foul temper, deep breath. Where is the puppy? I repeat, where is the fucking puppy?'

It's no wonder that they can't stay normal, they can't be themselves. What is themselves anyway? What is normal? That got lost years ago. They walk into perfect situations, they're handed the most delicious drink, the greatest snack, the room smells divine, everyone laughs at their 'jokes', everybody tells them they look gorgeous. Is that top new? Are you using that $200 face cream that got couriered by the PR? You look eleven! How are your children so divine? You're a magical mother. Here, sit down, would you like a back rub? Have you lost weight? Not that you needed to.

The seriously famous can't be like us, they can't be down to earth – it's simply impossible. Muggles/civilians/you and me aren't ourselves around them either, which seriously doesn't help. We're jumpy and trying to be memorable (embarrassing) or just quiet and staring (uncomfortable). We're warped, strange, like we are fifteen years old again and in the presence of someone we really, really fancy.

For the famous, this must feel odd, and to get over it they don't make eye contact with anyone. Walk past a megastar and they're always looking down, they're looking into the middle distance or they're in shades. It's not surprising – in order for them to stay sane they have to try to avoid seeing people's reactions to them. They close off from reality. And so they start to believe the palms and the wooden floor and the special salad is real life.

I suppose we have to stop expecting them to be normal as it's impossible. I'll tell you what keeps us all sane: having to wait, having to be uncomplaining, having to make do. Queuing for a coffee, spilling something on our t-shirt at 9.05 in the morning and realising we're basically wearing porridge on our top for the rest of the day, being late at the school gates, nobody handing us anything or telling us we're perfect, hilarious or beautiful. Having to be charming or apologetic or humble to our kid's teachers, our friends, the people in our lives. We have to work for laughs and we have to work hard for, well, work.

Famous people are not your dream dinner party guests. Forget your fantasy list and replace it with your true friends, people who won't mind that the moussaka is a bit overdone and the sponge is slightly undercooked. The megawatt stars should be applauded from the side-lines – see their movies, buy their records but don't end up in a room with them. You might find yourself laughing too loudly, getting the tea wrong and then will leave with a bad taste in your mouth (but that might also be the hideous seaweed salad).

Quite
INCONVENIENT

THEIR NAMES

I'm not usually someone who spends a lot of time thinking about themselves as it makes me slightly uncomfortable. I don't think there's a deep well within me that I need to understand and I'm generally too busy getting on with the stuff we all have to do. However, in this case, I feel some answers need to be sought.

The thing is, I want my kids' names everywhere. I don't have a piece of jewellery that doesn't have their initials on it and almost every bowl at home has their names painted on the base – even the bread board didn't get off unscathed as their names are chiselled into the side of it. My friends laugh at me, my husband thinks I'm weird and the children are mortified.

Each time I gave birth, once I'd turned 'Wonderwall' down, said thank you to the doctor and paid the manicurist (I'm only a bit joking) I had to be physically stopped from rushing to a tattoo parlour shouting, 'I want a massive J on my upper arm, or better yet, my forehead.' I didn't do it, but I still like the idea of having them stamped on me 24/7. If I'm talking about the foxtrot, chatting with friends over chips, mulling over the right way to say 'more to come' in a voice-over booth I'd like to look down and see their names, their marks on me at all times. This would be entirely embarrassing for them and is unlikely to be pleasing to the eye.

In place of tattooing myself, as they grew up, I felt compelled to get them personalised lunch boxes and t-shirts. I wondered if

I could put their names on their trainers (not just with a black sharpie on the inside). I'm about the only person who loves sewing those name labels into their uniforms. There it is, her name, his name. Maybe we'll put two name tapes on this coat as one is bound to fall off. Maybe I'll secrete a label into my own jacket too, when they're not looking. I just sit there with the needle and thread, smiling to myself. My fingers are sometimes bleeding (I have terrible eyesight) but I'm happy, holding tiny tapes with their names printed on.

I discovered one evening that I could order canvas holdalls from America with their initials on – quick, they're awake in Vermont and they'll ship! I'll call them and order immediately. And imagine my joy when notonthehighstreet.com started up. You can get names put on plant pots, Tupperware, Christmas stockings, the lot. I went bananas. Nobody had a jacket or a pencil that didn't have their name on it. In bold. We have an Arthur door stop (I'm being perfectly serious) and Matilda and Jake hooks in the hall (*what* is the matter with me). Their beach towels have their names on, as do little boxes that sit next to the bath.

I once had a meeting with a very impressive business person and explained that I wanted to give up television and just run a small shop that had an engraver and wood carver so people could come and order personalised butter dishes and blankets that could be monogrammed. That's right, he looked at me like I was unwell and told me to stick to reading out loud.

So why do I do it? Uncharacteristically, I've felt compelled to have a think about this. Is it perhaps a lucky thing? Is it really so they feel close to me? I'm a working mum so perhaps it's because I want to feel like they're somehow not far away, making me feel less guilty. But that theory doesn't really work as their names are all over the house, they're not just on my jewellery, they're everywhere.

The irony is that I hardly ever use their 'official' names, the ones on their birth certificates – I use Puffin, Puppy, Owl,

Sausage, Rabbit, whatever comes to hand. So why do I need to be reminded of them all the time?

I think, and I'm not being faux harsh here, that I'm bragging. Not really to others but mainly to myself. We made them, I gave birth to them, we have fed and clothed them and watched them get bigger and, not only that, I *like* them. We made nice people. But most of all, what I think it is, is that these three kids, each of their names, they're mine (for a bit) and they're at home.

It's a prickly truth and one I've only just worked out. I'm slightly mortified, embarrassed, ashamed. I thought that it was simply about me loving them, or even just liking their initials. But that really can't be right as my kids' initials spell out JAM. I know. It isn't even in my top ten of things to put on toast. Perhaps it's a good thing I didn't get that tattoo.

DEAR MEN,

In relationships, we sometimes say things we don't quite mean. We're not intentionally lying, maybe we just don't want the argument, or maybe we just don't want to explain. Explaining can be very strenuous. We might not want to hurt our partner's feelings so we bat something off and hope it disappears. Think of these as white lies then, sometimes little but other times … not. Here's a glossary.

'GO OUT, HAVE FUN'

You're right. I know what it sounds like. She's standing in front of you, she's saying 'Have fun!' You can see her mouth moving and those particular words are coming out. How sweet you think, she wants me to have fun. Uh, dude …

'Go barmy,' we say. 'Let it get really wild,' we encourage. 'We know you've worked hard all week,' we'll argue. We'll say you deserve a night out with your mates. We might help you get dressed, we may help you line your stomach (sweetheart, shall I make you a bit of toast?).

What we're actually saying is that we don't want to be the annoying wife/girlfriend/'ball and chain' who keeps you locked up indoors. Every group has one partner who's stricter than the others and the boys will laugh and poke fun. 'Allowed out are you?' and 'Do you need to check your watch?' and 'Will you have to get a permission slip if we go to a club?' and similar questions will be asked to much hooting. We don't want to be that person, that 'text me when you're there' and 'please keep your tracker on' nag. It's not that we think that woman is wrong (if she's that worried about something then yes, I'd say he's probably playing around) but we don't want the reputation. We want to be the cool girlfriend (outwardly speaking) who winks when you leave and promises a modicum of filth when you get back. I'll be here waiting babe, oh, and I got a new bra. That's what we want to be able to carry off.

What we'd like you to do is go out and slowly realise it's just not as much fun if we're not there. Sure, you'll get the drinks in and have a laugh, but then, when everyone is hammered and teetering off their stools and there's talk of the next bar or fast food, sneak off back home.

Don't be all 'But you said to enjoy myself!' Yada yada yada. Yes. Up to a point. Again, that's what we *said*, it's not what we *mean*. Just a teeny bit of fun. No more.

'DON'T WORRY'

We all do this, don't we? You explain you can't now make the parent/teacher meeting. You can't go to their work event because you've committed to seeing a friend. You haven't started cooking lunch even though you said you would because you're enjoying your book or the papers. You say sorry and your partner says, 'Don't worry' and you think, phew. That means everything is all right.

It doesn't though, does it? When she/he says, 'Don't worry,' it actually translates as, 'You should worry but I can't be bothered to tell you how you've let me down/got it wrong/upset me, so instead I'm going to answer like this. Because I don't want to have a row, because I can't get into it right now, because I just need to talk to my best friend to slag you off, because I fantasise about being away from here or about you being a different kind of person.'

We say 'Don't worry,' because we don't want to have to explain, out loud, why that is the wrong answer. When we say 'Don't worry' it means, um, worry.

'LET ME THINK ABOUT IT'

You want to invite your best friend and his new girlfriend round for dinner on Thursday? The night before the big presentation at work? You think that the fourteen-year-old wants to celebrate her birthday with a fishing trip where we all camp and cook on a stove using only a magnifying glass and some flint? You want us to enrol in a couple's palmistry course in the local town hall?

We nod and look at you and say sure, let me think about it. We really give the impression that we've slid that option/ idea into our brains and we're going to get right back to you. Christmas Day at your parents' instead of mine this year? Let me think about it. Spending our wedding anniversary at your best mate's because they've got a new bearded dragon? Let me think about it.

OK, here's the truth. We're not thinking about it. We're just biding our time while we work out how to explain why it's a bad idea and never going to happen. We never need time to think about anything. We have to move too fast – organising the groceries, feeding the cat, making sure the kids have done their art projects, calling back British Gas, earning a living, paying the window cleaner. We're quick as a flash, we move and make decisions at breakneck speed. We have absolutely no need of time to think about things. Remember that please. The next time you hear 'let me think about it' remove it from your head. It's a solid no. Plus, have you ever met a bearded dragon?

'WHY DON'T YOU ASK DADDY IF HE KNOWS?'

This isn't a gentle, 'Gosh I'm not very good at physics.' It means, 'Please get off the damn sofa/away from the TV/stop doing the fucking sudoku.' It means, 'I'm happy you're having a nice afternoon but I'm making gravy here and our kid (notice the *our*) needs help with their homework so FFS get involved.' But because it's Sunday, we will make it nice (we try to make everything nice on Sundays).

'I'M NOT SURE ABOUT THIS DRESS'

Right. Open your ears please. This doesn't mean I'm not sure about this dress. On any level, in fact, it's quite the contrary. What we'd like from you here is something lovely about our physical selves. Of course we're sure about the dress, we didn't buy it blindfolded, we didn't just chuck it at the till without looking at it, we're too smart for that. We asked our friends and we really thought about it. We weighed up the pros and cons, the 'will this still work in 2024?', we took photos of it, we have seen it from the back (a feat in a home without mirrors). We're absolutely positive we bang on nailed it but you haven't said we're pretty/attractive/sexy for a while and we'd like some attention please.

'THAT'S NEW'

Perhaps he bought a new picture for the walls. 'Look at this baby, got a nice big print, thought it could go in the kitchen. Yeah, you're right, it *is* a poisonous dart frog but really close up. Just love the mad colours, you know. Thought it was time we had something really bright in here.'

When the answer is simply 'That's new', it means we don't like it but don't quite know how to remove it and not hurt your feelings. We can also see that now, in the midst of the excitement about the new shiny thing, is not the best moment to express our alarm. We will save this for later and instead just opt for a 'That's new.' Our partner will do that too. Please see page 212 – when we got that hippo footstool and a cow butter dish (almost life-size), all he could muster was a tiny 'That's new.'

'IT'S LOVELY!'

You've handed over a present. You're proud of it. You might have really thought about it or you might have got it hungover on 24 December. Maybe you rushed into the shop and thought, 'Yeah, pink gloves. I've never seen her wear pink gloves, she's going to love them!' Or, 'An enormous book about the Ancient Greeks? Perfect. I am sure he once expressed an interest in the Trojan war.' If you hand it over and they open it and they exclaim rather too loudly, 'It's LOVELY!' then I think we all know that this simply means, 'Have you got the receipt?'

WHAT WE SAY, WHAT WE MEAN

So in conclusion, all relationships – and friendships too – require little fictions to smooth them over at times. We are busy, we are tired and sometimes we just know that now is not the right moment. As I think I have made clear, a lot of the time it's really no good being honest. That is not what is being asked of you. Here are some more things that we all say, and what we really mean when we say them. I think you will find them familiar.

WHAT WE SAY	WHAT WE MEAN
Thanks for that information	**Shh**
I'm so sorry I'm late	**I almost didn't come**
I'd love to do that	**Please don't make me**
I've just eaten	**I'm on a diet**
I think he's interesting	**Your new boyfriend is awful**
No, no, it looks good	**Don't wear it again**
Are you going to eat that?	**Give it to me**
He's a bundle of energy	**Control your son**
Where's that from?	**I'd like it for Christmas**
You're such an inventive cook	**This is inedible**
I'll check with him/her	**We're not coming**
What do you want for dinner?	**Please make it**

PICNICS

'Have you got the blankets, love?' comes shrilly out of your mouth as you sweatily search the back of the cupboard (behind the caraway seeds you bought in 2001) for some Tupperware boxes.

'Uh, have we got any?' he answers and you realise that yes, in fact you might not have any picnic blankets.

'Grab towels instead!' you reply with a lightness you don't feel as you realise your trying-to-be-a-1950s-perfect-housewife ponytail has budged a little to the left and you look like an ageing 1980s Bucks Fizz impersonator. You stand in the kitchen with mayonnaise everywhere wondering why you put a ribbon round your hair in the first place. You realise you're 48 and not Sandra Dee – mortifying. Someone has put some music on to accompany the prep and enforce yet more fun, so nobody can really hear each other. We're shouting 'DO WE HAVE ANY PAPER CUPS?' over the pounding noise. Not relaxing.

He appears with some fraying towels (mismatched, of course) and you don't dare ask about a cool bag.

It's the first properly warm and sunny day of the year and, without a doubt, across the country people are saying to each other, 'Ooh, it's a nice day for a picnic.'

There is almost nothing worse is there? To break it down, you spend all morning soaking hunks of meat in soy and ginger or shredding a cabbage – and I do mean *all* morning – and there's a certain hysteria in the house. If it was just, 'Sod it, let's make half-arsed sandwiches and grab some Pringles and sit outside till the flies drive us nuts' then fine, then a picnic would be entirely tolerable. But it isn't that. It's never that.

Picnics have to be magical. They have to involve small napkins and coleslaw (hideous when cold but actually satanic when warm) and gristly chicken drumsticks. There have to be accessories, such as a picnic basket – though if you have one that hasn't been filled with kids' toys, wires and adaptors, ancient school reports they'll never want to read or their old art offerings then call me, I need to understand you. And a picnic needs a ball, happy and grateful children, possibly a cricket bat (I know) or a skipping rope.

For some inconceivable reason we feel the need to hark back to some sort of imaginary summer's day we might have seen in the films. I don't know about you, but I didn't have picture-perfect picnics with my family when I was small, it's not like I'm trying to recreate something I had experienced and reminisce about. Yet, I get frenzied, it seems to all be based on the impeccable picnics I've read about in books, seen on a postcard, imagined in my head.

Picnics are stressful, they're a hassle. We aren't allowed to eat Twiglets on a bench for twenty minutes and call it a day, as that's not a picnic, that's a chat on an outdoor seat (which would be much nicer for all concerned). Everyone is being faux upbeat, a little too smiley (if your mouth hurts, it's not a real smile – first rule of happiness). Even if everything is picture-perfect. Even if you have all the equipment needed (and in that case you might just be a psychopath) – organic forks, food containers made of potato or turf and a beautiful big check blanket – you're still marching somewhere with a heavy box or bags and then sitting surrounded by other families pretending to have fun while dogs come and eat your food and toddlers take their sodden nappies off and chuck them on the ground.

After an hour of high-pitched, slightly desperate, 'Does

anyone want to try the prawn skewers? I sprinkled them with lemon zest!' you then have to pack everything up (sticky and warm now) and trudge back to the house, unpack and then spend ages trying to wash off the oily, greasy, mayonnaise-y residue that's on everything.

Picnics, then: a classic case of repeated behaviour that we should knock on the head. They are both a fantasy and a fallacy. We put too much pressure on ourselves to be the perfect unit on the perfect blanket eating the perfect food. Want me to tell you what's perfect? A bag of crisps at home.

THE GOOD BAD

There are lots of things people will tell you are bad, that we shouldn't feel, shouldn't do, shouldn't talk about, shouldn't applaud. These things are apparently negative, damaging and must be avoided. Well, I've been sent here to tell you that the following 'evils' are actually quite good news.

FAST FOOD

Oh no, we never eat anything from those establishments. Poppy here has never even heard of a McFlurry! We prefer everything to be homemade, we despise even the sound of a packet opening. Yes, you're right, it is harder work to make our own pasta and our own bread but why not? It's for our internal organs you see, we're just happier eating food straight from the ground or tree. That's clean living. Yes, you could say we're spotless in our eating habits. We only do organic and fresh and we've never gone to one of the large supermarkets. I mean, some of them have more than ten aisles. No, we favour the small and independent markets. We've been known to queue for an hour for a piece of chorizo. I'd rather die than let little Ludo have a Skittle, that's why we avoid most kids' parties.

There's a growing food snobbery that I can't really abide. Yes, fresh spinach is good; yes, it's excellent to support your local cheese/wine/fruit and veg shop and to eat healthily 90 per cent of the time but gang, have you never had an Egg McMuffin? Exactly, sometimes just nothing else will do.

BAD TASTE

We're always told 'tasteful' is minimalist and calm and un-shouty. People who have good taste choose well-fitting suits and their boots are always clean. They favour a crisp shirt (ironed) and a discreet mid-size, fawn handbag. People with good taste are softly spoken and keen on chocolate brown eye-liner and it's often said that once we're all grown up we should be more refined, more elegant, more neat.

Tasteful people are keen on soft background music, comfortable pale bathrobes, driving gloves and they think Vegas is vulgar. They have children called Tom and Anne and will inwardly tut if they overhear, 'Moonbeam, come on, it's time to go home,' at the swings. They have sensible pets (he doesn't shed and is groomed every Thursday) and matching luggage. They read their bank statements and they make sure they never crack open a new mascara, bottle of olive oil, pair of trainers until they're absolutely sure the old is completely used up and redundant.

People with bad taste like spicy food, loud noise, mismatched cutlery, *Dallas* reruns, sweaters with holes in and have kids called Chutney or Napoleon. People with bad taste swear a lot, scratch in public and sometimes wear tops that show their bra strap. People with absolutely no taste use too much mascara, wear large earrings and often have ramshackle drawers. People with bad taste wear seasonal clothes but in the wrong season. They'll throw on a summer dress with thick black tights in January. They're happy to wear heavy DMs in August. The only reason they choose something is because they *love* it.

Good taste, then, is highly overrated. You want to dress inappropriately and get lipstick on your teeth? You'll be more fun than Mr and Mrs Polite. Go for it.

UNPOPULARITY

Who wants to be the most popular person in the room? It does sound tempting. Everyone wants to talk to her/him; people literally stand in line at parties so they can just lap up some of that glow. She'll like me best! I'll tell her she looks fantastic, I'll mention her shoes, they look new. I'll be fast, can't waste her time but I'll try and say something memorable. The problem with being the most popular person in the room is that it's seriously hard work.

That person has to go to everything to keep their position, to keep being the most invited and the most fun. The number one in the room has to practically tap dance at dinners, they have to regale everyone with the best stories – people are looking to them to set the tone. They have to store gossip like little penguins so they can regurgitate it all up at the drinks, the Sunday lunch, the trip to the gallery. They can't turn up late in stained clothes and slump on the sofa with a girlfriend, yawn and eat all the snacks.

They need new clothes (can't wear the same thing at that many events) and new clutch bags and new ways to say the same thing. They need to know about Sienna (fabulous, you must go to such-and-such place and order the so-and-so pudding) and they need to remember everyone's kids' names. They need to never cancel and they need to be extra happy and freakishly upbeat.

Just writing this is exhausting, now imagine living it. I'm all for JOMO – joy of missing out (I have no time for FOMO). I want my friends and my gaggle to love me and so should you, but the whole room? Give it up. Let someone else have it who wants it more. You can say no to stuff, you can wear the same gear and you don't have to stand in the middle of the room at parties but can find a nook instead (this is the key to all of life).

GUILT

Here's something – there's absolutely nothing wrong with guilt. I'm going out again and not putting the kids to bed. I've just bought masses of food and walked right past that homeless person without offering anything as my hands were full and the car was on a meter. I know she's called twice but I'm really busy and will have to get back to her another time, tomorrow will be all right. Shit, I haven't spoken to my parents for a whole week, I should call.

These are all things we *should* feel guilty about and here's why: we are guilty. Stop avoiding the bedtime story, absolutely never walk past someone who is hungry and asking for food, call your friend back as if she's rung twice she needs you and ring your bloody parents because they love hearing your voice and it's the right thing to do.

That uneasiness, that qualm, that disquiet is a good thing. It's our heads, our hearts, our gut telling us we've been badly behaved. Of course these feelings of foreboding come in different variations – if you went to bed without putting a wash on then please don't sweat it, but you made somebody feel small or odd and didn't apologise, unquestionably get back out of bed and send a sorry. If you could help and didn't then yes, feel guilty.

People who never feel remorse are the ones who think they deserve 24/7 happiness, an easier life, sympathy. Beware of these people, they're usually narcissists.

You feel bad about something? Good. Guess what, you did something wrong. Sort it.

IMPOSTER SYNDROME

How on earth did I get this job? Why am I here? What if they ask me to speak at the meeting? What do you mean, I've been picked to do the presentation? What on earth are they thinking, giving me all this responsibility? What if they think I'm not up to it? I have to open the shop by myself? What if something happens? I've got six inches of make-up on, heels I can't walk in and I'm about to do this actually live on television. I have to hold onto (make that 'grip') his arm and walk down stairs and will then have to speak and people (they say) are watching.

When will they realise I can't do it? That they can get some-one much better? It's got to be any time now …

Imposter syndrome. When you think you're a fraud, when you think that you can't do the job. That niggling feeling that someone is going to find you out. The phone will ring. 'Ah, hel-lo, it's Lucy from HR. Well it turns out that little voice inside your head was completely right after all. All this time you've been thinking you weren't up to it? It took us a while to catch up, so sorry, so much admin up here, but you're bang on. You're nowhere near as good as we thought you were. It's time to pack up your desk. Please do so immediately, leave straight away and don't stop to talk to anyone.'

It's a slightly sick feeling, a just-waiting feeling. Here they come, they're here to tell me I've been too lucky, too jammy and it's all over. This feeling can of course come and go but it's always slightly there, humming in that little corner of your brain.

Here's the thing: I think a bit of imposter syndrome is in-credibly useful. It's good to ask, 'Why me?', it's tremendous to think this will end in disaster, it's excellent to question how you got there in the first place. Nerves, worry, a low-level 'I'm going to get caught out' makes us better at our jobs, it's as simple as that. I've met the odd person who believes they were meant to be there, that they were born for the role, that this was their rightful path, that the company is lucky to have them. You're right, total prats – not very popular, massive egos, hideous sense of entitlement and also (here's the funny bit) not always very good.

We have to make sure we don't take it for granted because the second we do, boof, it goes wrong. That work thing where you couldn't really be bothered to read the background notes – 'Watch me guys, this'll be easy peasy' – that's when it falls apart. Worrying a bit keeps us on our toes, it makes sure we turn up on time, smile a lot, work hard – that all comes from a fear of failure and as long as it's manageable and doesn't overwhelm we can really use it to our advantage. Keep thinking 'Why me?' and never rest on your laurels, that's just good sense. You can look back and say, 'well, that wasn't all bad' when you've retired but not before.

WATCHING TOO MUCH TELEVISION

I'm not just saying this because I work in it but here's some information.

Great television is good for you. Who taught me about animals? David Attenborough. Who teaches me about what's going on in the world? Emily Maitlis. I want to learn about different cultures, different viewpoints, I am so grateful to Louis Theroux for everything he's ever made. I want to laugh with my seventeen-year-old until we're sick – thank you to the team behind *Would I Lie to You?* and Matt Stone and Trey Parker. I want us all to sit down together and enjoy something as a family. Terry Deary, creator of *Horrible Histories*, we salute you. I want to see the Pyramid Stage but I don't actually want to walk a mile to use a portable loo so thank you Jo Whiley, Clara Amfo, Edith Bowman and Lauren Laverne. And I genuinely don't think I could have raised three children without the Teletubbies, the Octonauts and Mr Tumble.

The creative process behind each and every show should be applauded. It isn't chucked together, it isn't a last minute job. Michael Palin taught me more about the Sahara than I would ever have found out about in books and I knew next to nothing about Brunel before I tripped up over a documentary about him.

Television is our window to a world we might not otherwise see. Watch it, and learn from it, just by yourself or with your kids, and be proud of this, not ashamed.

ANGER

'Don't feel angry', 'Don't get all upset', 'Don't worry about it' and 'Let it go'. Good advice, yes? We are calm, mature adults. Let's not get in a tizz. Well, yes. But also, no.

I mean, don't get angry with the building works on your street or the temporary closure of a cycle lane. Don't get cross if the tube carriage is too full and don't get worked up if the last person who used the toothpaste didn't put the cap back on (slightly infuriated maybe, livid no), but if you do have a cause close to your heart, if you are worried about the plight of a group of people, if you think we're being governed by fools then sure, get enraged.

Fury elicits change. It makes us march, write to our MP, change the status quo. Throw off the 'I reminded you to buy yoghurt on the way home just TEN minutes ago' anger but hold on to the righteous rage. Being non-stop irate is probably bad for the body and soul but being utterly and wholly incensed about an injustice that you can help change is galvanising.

TEACHERS

I'm not a patient person. Where are my keys? Have you seen my phone? Did you book the hotel room? Have you told them we can't make it till 8.30 on Saturday? I'd like a tequila and soda please. Let me see your homework. Where did you put the mustard? What did he say about the raise? Put that back in the right place. Now, and I mean *now*. Faster. This second. Wait? No, I can't wait.

It's a bad attribute. I try to take it easy, to not worry about the speed of things but I'm extremely bad at it. Which is just one of the reasons why I am in awe of teachers; they are, simply put, the most patient group of people on earth.

You know when you throw your kids a party? Twenty-five kids over to yours for marmite sandwiches and some pass the parcel, a disco with a foam gun (thanks Uncle Ollie) and cake and blowing out the candles and here's a party bag. Remember the exhaustion, the looking at your watch and the where-did-I-put-the-black-bin-bags panic? Do you recall the overwhelming 'someone-pour-me-some-wine-and-put-me-in-a-dark-room' feeling that came over you the second the last child has been picked up? ('Sorry we're late, we lost track of time!' – WHAT?) And of course that promise you make to yourself at the end of every one: next time he can have two friends over and we'll get Dominos and invest in Disney+.

Well, teachers do that every single day, not once a year. They manage up to 30 kids all at the same time, day in, day out *all* the time. They have to like the naughty ones, the shy ones, the showy off ones, the nervous ones, the attention-seeking ones, the ones who never say please and thank you. They have to wait for kids to get their answer out while they nod and mutter encouraging words.

'Well done Luke for putting your hand up, the capital of France is …' (long pause, Luke is not quite sure, he's staring into space). If you're a teacher you're not allowed to answer, 'It's Paris, dickhead.' You aren't allowed to wail, 'But look at the board, Luke, there's the Eiffel Tower! We've just been talking about that city for *a full 30 minutes.*' Instead, you have to just smile and wait. When he finally says, 'Is it Brazil?' you're not permitted to roll your eyes or tut or laugh your head off or text a friend. Instead, you have to write in a small homework diary (that his parents might only sometimes glance at), 'More work on capital cities please! Have a fantastic weekend!'

You have to always be in a good mood and you can't be bored. These extraordinary people teach the same subject countless times. It's not just your little Jack they're explaining vectors to. They've done it every year. They've done it when it's sunny outside and when it's snowing. They'll have done it with the same enthusiasm. 'Welcome class, I'm going to teach you A level maths and I can't wait to get started.' And they mean it too. If you're ever had an excellent teacher (they're all excellent but some really get to you) then you never forget it.

So teachers of this world, thank you so much. We give you our heads and you fill them up and make them smarter and then some of us will put our kids' futures in your hands. You work so hard, you never forget to mark papers, you nod patiently when we can't quite remember something and you still encourage us and aim to inspire us. Thank goodness for you.

THE MOST WONDERFUL TIME OF THE YEAR

Which is the best time of year? I'm sure you've had this discussion with someone. Well, stand by, I am going to put it to bed once and for all.

Sure, blossom is beautiful and walking in crunchy leaves in October is captivating. Yes, there's a strong argument for Easter egg hunts (until you find a melted, slightly hairy chocolate ball at the back of the sofa six months later) and I know baby lambs are delightful. But without question, the most magical time of the year is of course Christmas.

People often complain that Christmas decorations go up too soon; I'd be happy for them to be erected in June. Christmas is all about sparkly lights, reindeer ornaments and the smell of hot food, which is of course really the key to life. There's no fennel or cold soup now, it's all blistering and possibly covered in gravy. Extra roasts for the table anyone?

The lead up to Christmas is great, on account of everyone being badly behaved and raucous and a little bit end-of-the-world mad. We eat too much, we sing carols too loudly, we say yes to everything. If March is your polite great-aunt then December is the naughty cousin who sneaks vodka in your drink when you're only thirteen. All bets are off. I missed the meeting/I was hungover at his nativity/I forgot to pay the bill as I haven't opened a letter since mid-November. All the rules, all the stuff that usually fills our heads as we rush around, just for a bit has gone.

Any lists we make are populated by items like brandy butter (is there a better invention?) and wrapping paper and the ingredients for Christmas cake. The house smells of satsumas and stilton and we forget about homework and sorting out drawers. The school rucksacks stay in the same place by the door for the whole period and washing from November gets damp in the laundry basket till January. It's impossible to be tidy at Christmas and this is deeply relaxing. There's stuff coming in (some mistletoe, a tree) and stuff going out (please deliver this present; I'll drop this box at the food bank) so neat and organised is put on the back burner.

As Christmas Day approaches, we get more and more sloppy and everyone makes joyous mistakes. In fact, the more you make, the better. Ha! I've burnt the toast. There are pine needles all over the kitchen and the hoover has broken. Never mind! The kids' presents get muddled up and now the seventeen-year-old might open a teddy and the eight-year-old will unwrap a massive Arsenal kit. No bother. Wrapping turns into a farce – babe, I've lost the Sellotape, pass me the Pritt Stick or fuck it, shall we use the stapler? Yes, of course eggnog is a good idea.

Everything is jumbled up and haphazard and better than Normal April and Organised September. There's anticipation in the air and the Christmas parties are loud bundles of happiness rather than the stiff outings of the rest of the year. Everyone is gently pickled and staggering around and they've slipped over on the way to the pub so they're covered in rain, snow or mud. Cold outside means huddled up and squashed indoors and everyone knows their bodies are undercover for the next four months so nobody is bothering about getting their toes done or waxing or passing up on macaroni cheese. People crowd round the bar and drink gin and eat small, slightly burnt sausages almost constantly. The office parties are disorderly and a laugh and nobody remembers what happened the day after. Even the people you don't love at work are shiny and weirdly fun and in a good mood.

I'm 48 and feel 110 but I still love Christmas Day. We wake up to squealing from upstairs – they've opened their stockings and are still unfathomably excited about a bruised clementine in foil and some out of date smarties. We see all our family, we eat till we can't move. There are games and everyone takes turns to cuddle my smallest nephew. My turn, we all shout as he lets us snuggle him and blow raspberries on his neck.

We only give stuff we can eat or use in the bath so it's basically shampoo or cheese. The kids are allowed toys and clothes but if you're over eighteen expect some caramelised cashews or hand cream. Better. Less stress. Someone dresses up as Father Christmas and hands out the wigs from last year (genuinely hilarious after a saddle of red wine) and we go to bed covered in crumbs and cracker hats. If the day is skewwhiff it doesn't matter. Some people are trying not to break garden chairs (sorry, that one is still covered in cobwebs), the bread sauce is found in the microwave after everyone has left, the Trivial Pursuit is from 1993 and nobody under the age of me understands the questions and as it's my mum's birthday we sing to her until we're hoarse.

Next is the time in between Christmas and New Year – the perineum if you like – and it's often the best bit. Absolutely nobody is getting dressed, no one is considering shoes and the house looks like someone has broken in and angrily thrown everything in the air. Did a typhoon rip through your place?

Nah, it's 27 December. Gotcha. It's like being a student again. Have you seen *The Young Ones?* Well, it's that. Nobody can remember when they last showered, it's 10am and mince pies are an excellent idea. While you're in the fridge can you pass me some butter? I reckon I'm just going to eat some with my hands.

The kids aren't stuck to their phones because the telly is so damn good – yes to watching a movie with turkey curry at midday. Slopped some rice and sauce on the sofa? Don't worry about it. Plus they're playing with their presents – a remote control car, a spirograph (completely compelling) and even the big ones are shouting over some Connect 4 and ice cream at 3pm. We're lazier than sloths and watch *E.T.* again (not up for discussion).

Now the only fly in the perfect Christmas ointment is New Year's Eve. Well, it used to be. When we were young it was the absolute epitome of high expectations ruining everything. You've been out before but this is it, this is the big one. Think you've been drunk in the past? Forget about it. Think you've snogged someone? That's nothing. Think you danced at that party in July? Oh, please.

That's how 31 December was when we were growing up. So much pressure, so much panic. Where will you be at midnight? I'm going to Balham, don't have the full address. Meet you there? Argh, it's 11.38 and I'm not in Balham yet. The whole thing was a mishmash of hell. What are you wearing? How are you doing your make-up? Who are you going to snog at midnight? Shall we crimp?

No night could live up to it; no evening could ever be that good. Simon le Bon is in your bed wearing only a Viking helmet holding a giant tub of butterscotch Angel Delight and he's going to sing 'Wild Boys' acapella while he kisses your thigh? Nah, New Year's Eve is going to be better, thanks. Then we grow up and all of a sudden it's just another night.

Now that we're older, it's different. We might wear slightly more eyeliner, something vaguely sparkly and we might buy nicer wine but we'll be with friends and we'll make it to 12.05

maximum. It's no longer a let down, a rush and scrabble for fun, a night of pain. It's just great and easy.

So yes, now I have explained, I'm sure you have accepted the self-evident truth of the matter. I know spring is lovely with its tiny chicks and, correct, the strawberries in June are delicious but there's actually no contest. If it's not December it's not fun.

DON'T EXPECT HIM TO BE YOUR 100 PER CENT

I know he's great. I know you trust him, I know he loves your parents and will stroke your back if you can't sleep. I realise you've had children and own a place together. Sure, he's the first person you'd have dinner with/go dancing with/play cards with. But still …

I know he's seen you at your lowest, your most raw, your most vulnerable. I bet he was great in the birthing room, when you lost your job and when you found out your parent wasn't well. You've been through a lot together.

But don't expect him to fill you up to the top.

If he's great, he'll get quite near the top. After a particularly close time – 'can I be honest with you' chats/fulfilling sex/a big old thing happening in one of your lives – he'll get bloody near. But it's unfair to think your partner can fill you up to the brim. You need friends and family and laughs and great boots and everything else in between. It's too much to think he alone will be enough – too much pressure on him, on you, on the relationship. The truth is, if he gets to near the 80 per cent mark then that's excellent – but you'll need to find the rest from somewhere else.

He shouldn't think you are all he needs either. OK, maybe we'd sometimes like to think they desire nothing or anybody else – not the football or the laughs with friends or the long chats with his family – but that's unfair and a hideous burden. Of course he needs those things, that's what makes him, him.

Love him or her and let them love you back. Be honest with them and listen to their worries and their hopes. Lie in bed all wrapped round each other laughing about when you first met and making plans for how the future is going to work (they want Eastbourne, you want King's Cross) and give them your whole heart. But please, they cannot be the only thing.

Quite
BOSSY

EYELINER

I realise this won't surprise you, if you've ever seen anything I've ever done, but I'm wholly uninterested in perfect.

I don't want polite and A* and 'bang on … I don't know how she does it'. I want ramshackle and holding it together and laughs and mistakes. I want to fail (have you ever seen me turn up at a black-tie event? Exactly) and I think we all put too much pressure on ourselves to be just so. We can't strive for perfection because we'll lose.

I don't want to make the perfect salad, I don't want to rear the perfect children (I will always think they are anyway), I don't want to have the perfect relationship. I've got very little time for the pressure that comes with it all. If the dressing is whisked and 100 per cent, if the kids all are always tidy and get firsts from Cambridge, if, after being together for 22 years, my husband rushes home every single night, kisses me and then makes tuna steak whilst humming Bob Dylan – what happens if something is a bit off? The dressing splits, the kids hate college and drop out, he comes home late and wanders into the other room while opening (and spilling) a bag of crisps. Basically, what if there are crumbs?

The house is immaculate, the pale pink angora throw is on the chair at the right angle, the flowers are in carefully mismatched glasses on the mantlepiece. The music is tasteful but cool and at just the right level as everyone lays the table while chatting about Dickens. Oh look, is that a crossword the teenager has started? Isn't it just superb he doesn't like being on his phone? Let's all complete it together. Tell us the clue to 10 down again baby, it's probably an anagram.

It's all so much. It's all, quite frankly, *too* much. Perfection isn't attainable or, if it is, something has to give. The working mother who always looks spotless, how does she have the time? The house that is 24/7 tidy, what's going on there? Don't they, uh, live in it? The family holiday that went without a hitch? Wait, no delays, no sunburn, no row about Scrabble? I don't get it.

If you're worried that everything won't be perfect here comes the rub. Get ready. Perfection is, when all is said and done, completely and utterly boring: a bit meh, a bit blah, a bit forgettable. Think of the people who seem to have everything going perfectly in their lives. Yes, those ones. Do you want to hang out with them? Be honest. They might serve the best Sunday lunches – I made two kinds of potatoes, don't hate me! You must try my chocolate fondant, they always come out right, no idea how! After all that, I bet you want to leave, I bet you want to run. The friend who only has good news – Life is amazing, the job is fulfilling, the kids all sleep twelve hours a night, I've never faked an orgasm. Is that someone you want to see? I'm not talking about envy here – you might covet their career or their lie in – but it's not just that: it's that perfection is dull. It's not fun, we don't want to be around it.

Allow me to illustrate further. Have you ever tried to create the perfect evening? Let's imagine that six people are coming round for supper. The house is bonkers clean, you scrubbed the skirting boards with a toothbrush and you've spent all day creating a picture-perfect curry. The eight-year-old is going to hand round crisps (hummus chips – you remembered to buy!) and the wine is chilled. The cheese board could win awards (how brilliant I bought figs) and the candles have been lit since five so the room smells like a tuberose field. They arrive and the conversation is good, no awkward moments, the food is hot and delicious and you finish with berries and cream and everyone goes home.

Whatever. I bet that wasn't your best night, the one you'd replay again. Yes, it went well but you were like a swan, manically kicking your legs while asking your husband to hand round the mango chutney with a smiley face. It's all too much effort, isn't it? You'd have got into bed not feeling full of joy but like you've just had a day at work, finished your thesis, been put on the spot. It feels fake, or at least somehow untruthful, not very you, not totally human.

The best nights are the nights that go wrong – you forgot to put the potatoes on so serve ice cold new ones by accident (you realise this once everyone has sat down); you used mint extract instead of lemon because you were rushing and have now created an actual toothpaste cake (this happened to me, we laughed, spat it out and it's still talked about five years on); the wine is warm because the fridge door doesn't fully close; the cheese that you bought in a panic smells like a giant's ball sack has been placed on the table. Everything is a bit disordered, a bit wonky.

The eight-year-old can't sleep because of the noise so curls up on a friend's lap. You laugh your heads off at your attempt to cook dim sum (they'd unfurled and were both a little bit burnt and a little bit raw) and you get into bed thinking, 'I have the best friends, I love my life, the kitchen is going to look like we've been burgled tomorrow, I need to get that fridge looked at. I will never, ever make dumplings again.'

This exact same principle is true of make-up and your general physical appearance. Not a hair out of place is not something I can get behind – it's not sexy at all. I'd like every hair slightly out of place, please. When it comes to eye make-up the scruffier the better. Use a good inch of your kohl to make the night worthwhile. Look like you've got ready in two minutes without the aid of a mirror and just don't stress about it. Perfectly applied highlighter is a bit worrying, a bit too headgirl. Chuck it all on and hope for the best.

I am helped in this by very bad eyesight – I had a prescription of minus 15 before an operation nine years ago and I still have not-quite-right eyes today. So if you have 20:20 vision stick your face on with the lights off and if you wear contact lenses please remove them before you get out your make-up bag. What we're after here is a blurry image, a sketch, an outline, a face that has been done with guesswork. That's hot, that's deeply casual, it's easy and it's mainly saying 'I'm not really that interested in what I look like, a mess will do.'

Flawless is vain, perfect is dull. Don't be that person. If you've got twenty minutes to get ready spend no more than three in front of a mirror holding a wand. You have much more to give, so much more inside you. Funny stories, chat, falling over, dancing, great conversation, hooting. The shell is just that – a shell. It's going to disintegrate in front of your very eyes. One day you're bouncy and OK and the next you're one of the Golden Girls (this is a positive btw) so your appearance – whatevs.

Also, the best nights end with even more mayhem on your face; your make-up at midnight is like a diary of the evening. You missed your mouth while eating chocolate mousse, you cried with laughter so your mascara is everywhere, you got caught in the rain because you forgot to order a cab before trampling onto the street because you were chatting with mates and now your hair is sodden. Basically, looking like you've fornicated in a puddle denotes a fantastic night.

What you do with the rest of your face – so long as it doesn't take more than three minutes – I can't comment on. And, as someone who likes to look like I've slept in tangerine gravy, I probably shouldn't try. You might be into something far more natural – go for it. I am a big believer in lip salve and have tried all of them (I know I exaggerate but on this I'm being truthful) and I'm pretty thrilled by eyebrow wands (the big fluffy mascara rod things, not the pencils – that takes precision which is something I don't have). But eyeliner – well, that is my area. So here you go. When it comes to eyes, I strongly advise you to do the following:

Put more on.

Yup, that's basically it. When you think you've done enough, when you're pretty sure you've piled on as much eye shadow as your eyelid can hold, I'd like you to shake your head at your bathroom mirror reflection and add some more. Rough it up and get it right into the corners, stick some kajal on the water line, maybe chuck on some navy or some sparkly stuff just to deepen it some more. Then, and this is crucial, mess it up. The key is to look like you've applied it three days before. It's got to be smudgy (the perfect cat eye – I'm allergic) and really rub your eyes after application and swirl the black everywhere. Use a brush if you must but I'd prefer you to use your fingers. Just make it mucky.

Don't use an eyelash curler unless you're into torture and high risk and put on more mascara than you think is healthy. Don't try using fake lashes at home (it's practically impossible and at the end of the ordeal they will still look fake) but invest in eyelash grow gel if you can be bothered. No, I'm not sure it works either, but you get a nice little placebo buzz after a couple of weeks – wow, they've grown. I look like Penelope Cruz.

So that's it really. Sometimes life gives you toothpaste cake when you were expecting lemon. Don't try to make things perfect, particularly not your face. Where your make-up is concerned, go with more, then some more, then mash it up. Balls to perfection. Class dismissed.

THE FRIDGE

I don't know how to even go about explaining the fridge situation in my house – or, in fact, how you can end up with 'a fridge situation' in the first place – but here goes.

Last year, I was in charge of doing up the kitchen. We decided that I would do it because it is completely inconceivable that we'd do something like this together. He'd have an opinion about where mugs would go and I'd instantly have to leave the room. Or him.

Maybe you're in a lovely relationship and can have adorable and calm chats about rugs and where to put some shelves. Maybe you lie in bed deciding between Le Creuset and Tefal pans. It's certainly possible that you spend the weekends moving furniture around your place casually discussing whether to get a floor light or a magazine rack or a new set of cushions. That's fantastic, that's lucky, that's lovely. That is, however, so very much not my husband and me. We have learnt the hard way that in our world someone has to take control and the other person has to smile and nod and accept how it is.

Twenty-one years ago, we got our first flat and thought that we'd decorate it together. How exciting, I thought; how romantic, he said. We'll wander round shops and look at wastepaper baskets and choose paint colours, we both gushed. We'll hold hands at Homebase like in the ads, I said, as we skipped off with a list of stuff to get – kitchen, bathroom, floors, paint, furniture, roof (yes, the flat was falling down). It was going to be super fun. Which toaster shall we get? A two-slicer or a four-? Shall we stop for a sandwich? Shall we do some kissing in Habitat?

That is not, I repeat *not*, how it worked out. We have very different ideas about houses (we were together for about eight minutes before getting married, it had never come up). I know what I like – wallpaper, cosy, big chairs – even if I have no idea how to choose it or arrange it, whereas he is Danish. In practice, this means that if he's not talking about Copenhagen then he's telling me about a Viking stool that's been made from one piece of pale wood by someone called Sven. He likes colourless, understated, whitewashed. You know all the hygge stuff? Pale pale pale, maybe with a fur throw and candles lit in the day? That.

By the time we'd finished buying stuff for that first flat together it looked like it was having a fight with itself. Green jungle wallpaper (also on ceiling) with rugs and too many pillows (me); white walls, white shelves, white desk (him). Every time anyone walked into a different room (there were only four) they thought they'd had some sort of turn, a spell. Wait, is this the same place? There's a grandfather clock in this room and one million trinkets but in the other room there's a digital projection on the wall and an oar leaning against the doorframe. Well, quite.

When we moved into the house that we live in now, we faced facts and decided to simply take it in turns. Whenever something needed doing just one of us would handle it – sometimes it would be him, sometimes me. A decade ago, it was his time, it was his deal. So he went to B&Q and he chatted to the builders about which particular white he wanted on the walls, on the floor, in the bathroom, for the tiles. Don't panic, it turned out it was all the same white, he didn't even want different shades. I mean …

Still, we didn't argue and I was appreciative he was doing it, knowing the second I suggested some William Morris fabric or an embroidered wall hanging it would all go downhill. 'Off you go babe, keep going,' I said. He basically created a white shell and then put white things inside it. I liked it, it all worked, it was considerably less visually confusing than our flat had been, but I need to tell you about the kitchen.

I'm going to be serious for a minute – it was a heady mix of dentist surgery and space station. It didn't have actual buttons anywhere (hidden you see, very Scandinavian) but if someone had appeared and said, 'Two minutes to take off, Sir,' or, 'She's on her way and she needs urgent root canal,' nobody would have batted an eyelid. It was white, it was wipe down (we had small children by then) and that was that. There was nowhere to sit apart from four (white) make-up chairs that he'd found, presumably in a make-up department. And one wooden monkey that was hanging off a white shelf in the corner.

Eleven years later, after a lot of wiping down and semi-successful stain removal and creaky cupboards that didn't close any more, it was my turn. I have mentioned how bad I am at anything to do with interiors, so I asked my clever friend and she suggested sofas and chairs and window seats and maybe books. Yes! Books everywhere, I said. And colour on the walls. Yippee, I thought and spent an awful lot of time choosing foliage and rugs.

I searched for large salad bowls for a solid three months. I'll get a new container for tongs and wooden spoons, I thought. This is really terrific. We should all do houses, we should all do kitchens; I'm chucking out this pan from university and getting a new one for eggs. Maybe *Architectural Digest* will call. 'Hello? Ah, you've heard about it, my tropical forest and busy kitchen? Of course you can come and look at it. Aniston wants exactly the same? Understood.'

It was all going well, things started arriving – trestle table, new fruit bowl, some rugs, a couple of chairs, pink glasses. Oh look, the plant man is here, help me get these in, babe. I subscribed to the *New Yorker* – so nice to have about – and

I couldn't wait to fill the green vases. He took it all very well and said 'nice' and 'lovely' every time something new arrived at the door. More non-white furniture? OK, he uttered. (His Danish heart must have been quite tearful at this point but he remained upbeat.)

Everything was there, everything was fantastic, the tortoise (yes, we have a tortoise) was happy as he'd never seen so much colour, so much greenery. However, there was a problem. In my excitement I had simply forgotten about the bit of the kitchen to do with food. Sure, I'd chosen an oven and a cupboard but that was basically it. 'Oh, I see,' I said, trying to sound brave. 'Well, we only really eat roast chicken or bakes anyway and we do have an oven, look!' I finished brightly.

Have you ever been inside a nursery school? You know they sometimes have those little wooden kitchens in the corner? The kids can put stuff in the fake oven and play with the pretend fish slice. That was basically what I ordered. Everything was fine though, we were still smiling and all was dandy. But then the fridge came. You've seen a hotel mini-bar? Great, now you see the problem. To be specific, we now have a fridge that can fit at any one time the following:

- 1 pint of milk

- 3 Diet 7up cans

- 1 piece of cheese (small)

- 1 onion and maybe a cucumber (there is no space for kale – I'm not sad about this)

- Maybe either some fish or some chicken. Up to four single prawns

- A pat of butter (if we put it on the tiny shelf in the door, but this does mean it falls to the ground every time you open the fridge)

Now, I love the whole room so I'm not complaining, but the family do. All. The. Time. There isn't space for ice so they ask for cold drinks almost constantly; they question whether the carrots will be a bit warm and floppy again (they really do get a little limp) and if more than three people want to eat at one time we have to rely on baked beans. They send me photos, my husband and the big kids, of fridges. They like the massive ones with huge levered doors. They regale me with stories about their friends who have extra freezers just for fish fingers and ice cream.

I would like to take this opportunity to say sorry. I'll fix it one day, if I can just work out where the plants should go, and in the meantime I'm so happy I've given you all something to laugh at, to roast me for. Come to our house you all say when we're out, we can cook you a singular rasher of bacon, we can make you a tiny slice of tomato. Ha ha. How you laugh. It's good to be able to take the mick out of your mum, it's bonding, it's important. So I suppose what I'm also taking this opportunity to say is, you're welcome.

THE WORST KIND OF PEOPLE (YES, I'M TALKING ABOUT PARENTS)

You'll be at the office minding your own business on a Monday morning and suddenly you're hearing all about little Jack's weekend. You haven't asked, you didn't bring it up. You're just standing there waiting for the coffee machine to kick in, you're wondering if it's too early to eat your lunch and you don't particularly care if he can now say meerkat or if he enjoyed the soft play ball pit but it seems you're hearing about it anyway.

You might be on the train looking forward to a bit of a daydream and a word game on your phone. You've got a front-facing seat, a small table, a bag of mini caramel waffle biscuits and someone that you don't know starts talking excessively loudly about little Tommy's new obsession with dinosaurs. 'We just can't get over it! He loves them! He even knows which ones roamed the earth in the Cretaceous period. I mean, is he a genius or what? Dinosaurs? At his age! Can you believe it?' Uh, yeah, I can believe it, all kids love them. Please turn it down.

The 0–18 phases go like this: anything brightly coloured (babies have absolutely shocking taste, don't waste your money on anything in heather grey or lemon yellow, they want crimson and electric blue, it's a scandal), teddies, Peppa Pig, Play-Doh, bugs, cars, dinosaurs, unicorns, football, princesses, music, slime, make-up, beer, dancing, boobs, penises. They might skip one or two or maybe they'll swap the order but that's pretty much it.

Parents talk about their kids 24/7 and if they're not talking about them you should know they want to be. Even if they're looking at you and listening to your plan to visit Costa Rica and they're nodding while you're talking about your mum, and their mouth goes into a perfect O while you're gossiping about your boss, know that they're waiting like a hawk. They're making eye contact, they're sympathetically cocking their head to one side, but you should be aware they're mainly wondering how quickly they can get their phone out to show you a photo of their offspring. They're working out how to turn 'I'm really worried about my dad – he keeps forgetting things' around so that they can casually mention how Lily can now ask for a drawing pin and a ticket to Lyon in perfect French.

Parents then, are all pretty ghastly. And almost without fail they fall into two categories. Those who push their children. And those who don't.

The Pushers are always in a rush. 'I'm just taking him to judo, got to make sure I've got his belt. Did I say it's a black one? Oh I *did* mention it? Ha! Just the three times? Sorry about that, thing is, he simply has an aptitude for it – he doesn't get it from me! Then there's a swimming gala on Friday. I've told him not to worry about coming first in the butterfly but does he listen? It helps that his dad is the coach, of course.

'He'd love to have a play date but we've got to fit in some time for extra maths, you see. Pythagoras really can be an uphill struggle, can't it? We did show him the basic rules of pi when he was two, rather miraculously some of it went in! That whole flashcard game can't have been a total waste of time, could it? Gosh, timing everything can be so tricky. If I didn't have my home-laminated extra-curricular timetable I don't know what we'd do. We're giving him at least fifteen minutes to meditate on Saturdays but otherwise it's go, go, go.

'He has to write thank-you notes to his teacher, learn how to eat with a fish knife and he needs to make his bed with military precision. Do we inspect it? Course we do. Got to run, he's about to take part in an online chess competition and hasn't quite grasped the full potential of a bishop. Chat another time!'

That's the extreme. We've met those parents and we've avoided them but then again we've completely relied on them for the 'When's prize day again?' and 'Look, I promised to bake a cake for the tombola but I've got a crashing hangover, so while you're making your Fabulous and Fancy Fruitcake do you mind bunging some brownies in the oven as I've got to fry some bread in butter and then get back into bed?' moments. But that's about it. We don't make eye contact if we don't need to.

The Non-Pushers are much more relaxed, almost horizontal. When it comes to their kids they're completely allergic to using the word no. 'My cherub can do whatever he wants, whenever he wants. Is he learning an instrument? Hell, no. I just don't want the hassle of the practice, to be honest. He needs to be able to unwind. I want him to come back from school and just slump in front of the TV. Sports? Well, we're hardly Olympians. I think it's good if he doesn't get too competitive. He doesn't need us taking him to the park to play catch. He's only eleven and I don't want him to fail. We always tell him he's our perfect baby and we give him a secret medal for whatever he does, so it's win-win really.

'We don't tend to have a timetable for anything, life's too short! We don't have strict bedtimes or reading times or any of that nonsense. Plus, I don't want to have to police him, do I? Do this, do that, practise your spellings. Who cares what he gets in Spanish, seriously, we're not moving to Barcelona! No, our little fellow can go on his iPad and play games and just be. Why should he keep his room tidy or tie his own laces when he has me? I love doing everything for him, he really is an angel.'

So the question is, which group are you in? Or, if you don't have kids, which do you think is right? Correct, bang on. Minus the madness of course, your kids *need* to be pushed. I just want them to be happy? I'll tell you when they'll be happy. When they get As, when they get a good job, when they try. They'll be happy if they have enough sleep, if they can add up and if they're taught manners.

Mine don't play musical instruments and I'm not a big believer in clubs (Dungeons and Dragons might be fun but, though I don't like to think about it, at some point they're going to have to lose their virginity) but I think a push is helpful. I think a nudge is sensible. I haven't birthed friends, I've birthed small people that should be able to read a newspaper and talk about it afterwards, do long division, put a wash on, carry out their chores and say please and thank you. I have no interest in grumpy, phone-playing, grunting kids who get everything they want. I want them to work hard, to listen and understand, and to follow certain rules. And yes, you're right, I'm extremely unpopular at home.

I love them, I kiss them, I cuddle them and they're the loves of my life but do I simply want them to think they're fabulous all the time? No. I've met those kids and I don't want to live in a house with them. I don't expect mine to do every afterschool activity going, but I do want them to be interested, to ask questions, always ask to leave the table, make their beds and deal with it when they lose. Go to sleep early, get a book from the shelf, put some toast in for everyone if you're making some for yourself and write thank-you cards even if you hated the present.

Parents – you have my permission to push. Their partners and friends will thank you for it later.

DO IT IN BLACK

You've read the what's hot lists, you've seen the fashion pages. They say full colour is in, they say everyone who's anyone is doing it. You nod, you find anything in your cupboard in the colour of the moment as you want to be on trend, dressing for right now. So yes to the fluoro orange sweater. Hooray I kept those electric blue cords. Let's look like the girl on the cover of that magazine. All the colour, all the shades, I'll feel so Liechtenstein, so on trend. Ladies and gents, I'm going to brighten up my life, you say.

Then you're out of the house and on the bus and it suddenly occurs to you you're going to work dressed as Mr Tumble. Hello there, Madam, do you earn your living dressing up as a clown at kids' parties on the weekends? Do you have one of those fake carnations in your button hole that squirt actual water? I bet you're a right hoot once you've had a gin! Colour, in truth, screams 'I'm fun, me' and that, my friends, is how to feel spectacularly un-fun. It was a good idea at 8.50am and now it's 11 and you feel too loud, too much, too jolly.

Be funny, be amusing, have all the one-liners but please, do it in dark colours. Life is about lowering expectations, so let them think 'This one in her big black coat and her black boots and black jeans will be a bit down, a bit dull' and then wallop – you can be light and airy and fizzy without the burden.

Colour is for the under-10s. If you're reading this and you're nine then go ahead, match that shocking pink velour unicorn hoodie with yellow daisy jeans. But if you are older, then pack it in. Black, navy, heather grey are your friends. Let the world think you're quiet and slightly moody and a bit glum and then be the life and soul.

If you glean anything from my witterings then please let it be this – wear black. Never feel like you need to 'jazz it up' (and let's never use that phrase out loud) with a bright belt or a colourful hat or an upbeat red bolero. Black is cool, black is hot (yes, at the same time – this colour literally breaks science). Even if you're not feeling up to dealing with the whole day – meetings, chats, people, traffic, smiling, lunch, the supermarket – if it's all a bit of a headache everything will be easier if you're in black. You can handle it, you're winning, you've got everything under control. Because whatever happens, you look bloody brilliant.

Black says yeah without being offhand. It says 'I know what I'm doing' without being boastful. Black says chic without needing to be actually French and it says ageless without being boring. Black is the king of fall-backs too. Can't decide what to wear, what goes with what? Put on all black. Can't really handle pairing separates – argh, does this cream shirt work with this brown blazer? All-over black gets rid of all of that. Black is mysterious, it's deeply unflappable and effortless, even when you're making an effort. Be exactly who you already are, but do it in black.

IN PRAISE OF (ALMOST) NOTHING...

A great partner, knockout friendships, good health are the big ticket items, the things we all hope for. But let's not overlook the fact that life is also about the tiny, the small, the reduced. Those little things that are easily overlooked, and might even sound trivial to someone else, but that can really make your day. You will have your own list – if you haven't already written it down then I think you should. Right now. It's always good to know and to have to hand what can make you happy, even just in the short term, on a Tuesday in February when you think you might be coming down with something. While you're thinking about it, here's mine ...

A GREAT OMELETTE

You can have your fancy towers of sea foam, you can queue for an hour for extraordinary brisket. You can jump up and down if you're going to a place that has the word 'gastronomy' on the menu. But when all is said and done, the best meal on earth is egg and chips. That's just a fact, end of conversation, new paragraph.

If you want an alternative (mainly because it's impossible to make great chips at home), can I strongly suggest an onion and cheddar omelette with crispy new potatoes? I know, I know. This wasn't supposed to be a cookbook but if I didn't include this recipe then frankly what good is any of it?

First off, get miniature new potatoes and put them in a really hot oven after covering them with oil and salt. Don't dribble anything: pour. Fry the onions extremely slowly, like there's no rush (there's always a rush but don't hassle them, pretend you're cool about them taking ages – you do you, onions, no bother) and then whisk at least three eggs in a glass or bowl and add salt and pepper and pour this over the super-soft onions. Add chunks of mature cheese (grate if you don't find it painful – I find it painful) and then grill (if you can be bothered) or flip it over in the pan (though this will be messy) and eat with the potatoes straight from the oven. If this doesn't make your heart skip a beat then you must never call me.

NEWSPAPERS

I don't know where I'd be without the papers. Lost probably. The weekends are great because they're weekends but my highlight is racing round the corner and coming back with the papers. I'll start with this section, you take that. OK, now let's swap. I inhale every bit even though I know absolutely nothing about business or property.

Journalists or newspapers are easy to poke fun at, or complain about – all they do is fixate on who's going out with whom, right? They're so keen to give us their point of view. We've got the internet now, not sure I need a paper. Wrong.

Sure there might be stuff about J. Lo's abs or Tom Cruise's body. They're filling space and I don't mind it. This book might be reviewed (hopefully not) and they'll tear it to pieces or I'll wear something disgusting on a TV show and will get laughed at. I get it.

Of course newspapers assume different positions on the political spectrum, but you can choose which suits you and read that paper. And also – perhaps even better – you can choose to read one that's on the other side. You'll be alarmed, you'll be raging but you'll know what you're up against.

Investigative reporting is so important, it's absolutely vital for now. Holding truth to power is essential and we'd be lost without it. Journalists get behind the story, they check underneath the curtain. They are the people who are ensuring that those in authority are doing what they say they are and who hold them to account when they're lying.

I promise I'm not just adding newspapers to this jaunty list because my mum worked on Fleet Street, though she did used to tell me when I was little 'we're just trying to find the truth'. When I was really small I never knew what that meant but as I grew up and I saw her tussle with those in power, encouraging brilliant writers to find out who was untruthful and who was doing the right thing I realised how important it is. The papers – absolute highlight of my day. They cost a quid (and are excellent with a cheddar and onion omelette, see previous page).

SAYING I DON'T KNOW

'Actually, I don't know. I haven't made my mind up yet. I need to read more on the subject.' I'm so pleased when I hear someone say this. It's fine, admirable even, when people don't know.

When did we have to become all knowing? When did we begin pretending to have all the answers? Why can't we admit we sometimes have no idea? Try it when you next have a chat with someone. You're at a dinner and everyone has a strong opinion. What do you think about such and such? It's definitely this, it's definitely that. They get worked up, heated, they absolutely *know* they're right about something.

It's the same on Twitter, no room for nuance. It's this – no, no, you're wrong, it's definitely that. In real life it's absolutely OK to say 'I'm not sure'. It doesn't sound thick – quite the opposite.

ORANGE

If you are naturally pallid with a soft blue-like tinge like me then you might believe that pale is more interesting. I get that you might find fake and fluorescent a little disgusting, a bit cheap, a bit obvious. I can pretend I'm like you, that I want to be chic, but the truth is I am a massive fan of bright carroty faces and limbs.

I fell in love with looking like I'd washed my face in Minute Maid when I was fourteen. I was extremely pasty (I still am – left to its own devices my skin is transparent) and I tried my mum's Ultra Glow (a very 80s product – think bright orange powder in a pot). There was a ginormous brush and a large palette of sparkly russet powder just next to the sink. 'I'll have a bang on that,' I thought. I played and played and when I heard the call for lunch – 'It's mulligatawny soup, come' – I entered the kitchen and everyone fell off their chairs screeching with laughter. You know George Hamilton? Yeah, double that. And then times it by 100.

It didn't put me off. I felt healthy, glamorous, like the girls in the ads, like the models on the beach in the Next catalogue. So shimmery, so dewy, so grown up. From then on, I would use anything to give me the glow (my mum quickly hid the good stuff). I'd use old tea bags to give me what I was after, I would ask for fake tan for Christmas and birthdays and never got over the addiction. If I feel at all down or slumpy (spellcheck told me this is not a real word but I'm sticking by it) a hefty whoosh of bronzer perks me right up again. I'm like a plant who needs the sun, only I don't need the real sun, just cream or spray or mousse that will slowly dye my skin. Gravy granules are a good alternative if you've run out of blush.

Loads has been written about how to get rid of the lizard bits when the tan starts to fade, but don't worry about expensive erasing foams and loofah sponges. Just put some table salt in the bath water, have a soak and use a pot scourer on your feet, elbows, hands. Get out of the bath, dry and reapply.

HP SAUCE

Ketchup is sweet but a little bit meh.

Mustard is good but not all the time.

Salad cream is perverse.

Mayonnaise is often … just too mayonnaisey.

HP, then, is the king of all condiments. If you don't believe me then put this book down and immediately walk to the butchers to get some sausages. Cook them in the oven with a bit of salt and honey and then dip once scorched.

See?

SCENTED CANDLES

If there's a single item that illustrates we've all gone completely tonto then this is it. Yes, they're just wax cylinders that smell of musk/fig/roses. They're literally just coloured glasses full of scented paraffin. We could get a tea light, a fake candle, we could dim the lights, we could turn the hob on for that fairylike flicker but we don't. Instead we spend a week's wages on globules of scented wax. I'd love to say I'm above it but I can't – I'm afraid I'm a full convert.

When they started appearing in fancy shops and people got excited, sure, I thought it was absurd. But then I went to a house that smelt of a flower stall and boof, that was it. I was won over. If you've had an odd day, if you're trying to control the noise in the kitchen and in your own head and you want to make yourself feel better then light one. This can just be for five minutes (I will never comprehend the people who light them for four hours, I mean, just stick 20 quid in a fire, love) and the room smells fantastic and suddenly you feel very civilised, very grown up, very in control, very modern.

'Babe, what are you doing?'

'Well, I felt like crying or having a shot of vodka and I've lost my phone and the keys and the kids are arguing and I forgot to cook the chicken yesterday so it's gone off.' (beat) 'But everything is sort of fine now because the place suddenly smells of cinnamon and amber.'

NEW PYJAMAS

When was the last time you bought a pair? I did a ring around (let's call it research) and none of my friends, not one, has bought anything new to wear to bed in the last twenty years. We all wear the same t-shirt, the same nightie, the same old tatty thing. We might get into bed naked (though this usually stops at 40) or we might just wear the nearest thing we can find after a long day – some Minnie Mouse shorts from our daughter's laundry basket and his vest because we never, ever buy ourselves nightwear. You might have got a new massive white tent for the hospital birthing room (I wore my mum's that she wore when she had me, this is either disconcerting or lovely – you decide), but in terms of buying something specifically for the purpose of wearing it to bed – nope, we don't do it.

So can I casually suggest going into M&S and getting yourself something new to wear at night? I did it last year, it feels massively extravagant. You'll be excited about getting under the covers daily. Go silky if you want; I'm a fan of anything flannel.

DISABLING YOUR VOICEMAIL

Right then. This small thing, this work of seconds is a game changer. That notification 'you have three messages'; the text that keeps reminding you that you have a new voicemail and you tut, turn the phone over and put it off. You finally have a listen, but you can't delete it until you've heard three seconds. Come on come on. Still going. This message is from last Thursday and it's from my husband asking if I want something from the supermarket. Well, yes, right this second I want some lettuce for the tortoise and some eggs. Getting this now, however, four dates later, is not useful. Disable your voicemail this second.

Someone rings and can't leave a message. Guess what? They'll text, they'll email. You'll see a missed call. Let's get rid of the clutter, let's throw out the extras, let's free up some time. I did this only yesterday and if I didn't have a dodgy knee, an old back, glasses constantly on top of my head as well as on my face I'd do a cartwheel. Voicemail is so last decade. It's time to move on.

BABY GOATS

Have you ever met a baby goat? A real live one?

I met four in 2015.

We were on a hill in Switzerland (true life) and these tiny little creatures came up to us. I'm a fan of small animals generally and can talk for hours about my adoration for baby otters, small puppies, newborn owls (seriously) but can I suggest that when the day takes a turn, when the world feels a little dark, immediately get onto a search engine and watch baby goats gallivanting about in a field.

More uplifting than a massage, a sound bath, a glass of wine or a deep breathing exercise.

CARPET

Yes, I know floorboards are fashionable and I know they look good.

'Oh, you got new floors. They're very nice. Aren't they pale? Aren't they dark? Yes, very chic.'

'I saw them in that interiors magazine and here they are. We look after them really well, they have a special polish. Here, smell the polish.'

Cool, great. When we're done with congratulating ourselves on our artily distressed or super-polished woodwork can I just praise the majestic carpet?

You get out of bed at 7am in November. You know what you want to put your feet on? Correct, fluffy floors. You pad around the sitting room before bed looking for the book you started and have now lost. Want me to tell you what will make the search more fun? Correct: cosy, furry flooring. We can all be cool when we're out (shades, lipstick, visible bra strap, drinking shots) but what we want to come home to is shedloads of carpet. (Quick note: sisal is absolutely not carpet, it's like Weetabix on your feet.)

LEFTOVERS

I love restaurants but I fear they're missing a trick. Nice clean dishes, freshly plated food, a perfect chicken breast, some green fronds, a side order of broccoli. All delightful, all to be admired. There's been a lot of shouting in the kitchen, 'Yes chef!' and 'Two chickens, one beef and one lasagne for table four' and I absolutely love them for doing all that and bringing it to us. But I think we are all aware that the best food is the stuff kids leave on their plates. A half-eaten fish finger, some corn that didn't quite make it in the mouth, some sticky pasta sauce and some only-glanced-at cauliflower cheese.

The restaurant I'd like to go to would be just that. You arrive and pick your kid – 'I'll take Max please, table three.'

'He's been given fish pie, some peas and carrot sticks. If you just wait here, Madam, he'll be done in about three minutes. He's had a good go on it but now it's time for him to go to the soft play area. And your friend here, will he be interested in Lucy (spaghetti and meatballs and a Shirley Temple) or Frank (a kid's roast, hold the bread sauce). Ah, Lucy, fantastic. We'll seat you in ten.'

And that's it. Their plates are taken from their high chairs and brought over with great pomp. Who ordered the Mary? Right. Here are some chipolatas and gravy and she didn't touch her mash. Enjoy your meal. This would be my dream restaurant and if someone could sort it that would be excellent.

————

So there you go. That's my list. Just a few generally underrated things that make a difference to me. I hope your career is going well, that your toddler has finally stopped screaming every time he is put in the high chair, that your mum is on the mend. But if it's not, he hasn't and she's still under the weather, then can I suggest consulting your own list and perhaps just enjoying something that makes you happy on a small scale for five minutes, an hour? And if all else fails, well, all I can do is say it again: baby goats, guys, baby goats.

JACKIE COLLINS

Do you sometimes feel meek, embarrassed, a little bit small?

Do you stand in a queue for an hour, get to the front and then apologise to the girl as she tells you they've just closed and you have to go back the next day? Of course, silly me for getting here so late. Do you tell the dry cleaner that it's actually not a problem that they ruined your new dress because you wanted an excuse never to wear it anyway? Thank you so much, you've saved me from some decision making later. Can I pay by card?

If your boyfriend says he's going out (again) and will probably stay in the Holiday Inn round the corner so he doesn't wake you up when he gets back at 4am do you nod and say that's actually fantastic and extremely thoughtful? Do you help him get ready for his big night – no, wear that shirt, you look really sexy in it. Don't worry about the hangover, I know you'll be monosyllabic and grumpy all weekend. Tell you what, I'll make your favourite food and give you a foot rub while you watch the football. Love you! Bye!

Do you tell the father of your children that it's wonderful news he's last-minute swapped the weekends he's looking after the kids as that night out you had planned would probably have been too raucous anyway. Have fun in Ibiza! You leave them with me and we'll go to the park in the howling rain again. No problemo.

Is any of this you? Even slightly you? Do you people please until you don't know who you really are any more? Do you want everyone to love you so much you'll do anything to make it all OK? Do you try to fit in a bit too readily, not getting in the way, because you don't want to be 'difficult'? Do you say you like everything – all the different ways to eat eggs, dark walls, light walls, high ceilings, cosy low ones. I like it all, no preference from me! Everything is fantastic!

Do you thank your boss for calling you in the middle of a family Sunday lunch to ask you to go into work to check something that could easily be checked tomorrow? While you're there, do you sort out the mugs and the coffee area and water the plants?

When your child's friend punches him in the lunch queue, do you tell his mum at the school gates that it was probably your kid's fault? Do you apologise profusely on his behalf and say he no doubt deserved it and can be a right pain!

Basically, do you sometimes think you're wearing a 'Please Like Me' t-shirt, happy to fold in with everyone else's plans? Have you maybe forgotten if you prefer the cinema, a night in the pub or just staying in? Where are *you* exactly? Are you a tiny bit lost?

I mean, I'm exaggerating here, but if any of this (even a little bit) sounds like anything you ever do, then can I suggest you channel Jackie Collins?

I interviewed Jackie Collins once and she was a total knockout, a brilliant woman with a great laugh and her priorities straight (I'm not sure how I gleaned this from a twenty-minute chat either but sometimes you just know, don't you). She lived in a house predominately designed in animal print. She had leopard walls, zebra floors and faux tiger throws. She was wearing an animal print blazer and was extremely glamorous. For all her smiles and kindness – sit anywhere! Here, let me get you a drink – she also had a strength, a purpose, a presence. Was she fun? Sure. Had she sold more than 500 million books (read that figure again)? Absolutely.

What we learn from Jackie is simply this: know your worth. I do realise it sounds like a hideous inspirational quote but they're not *all* wrong. So what I suggest is that if you can't quite locate 'you' in all the clamour right now start by dressing with a bit more muscle, a bit more control, a bit more authority, and consider embracing animal print.

It doesn't have to be top to toe, it doesn't need to be your shoes, your jacket, your beret (don't wear a beret please) and certainly don't buy an actual tiger onesie, but dressing like Jackie will give you a bit of oomph. It can be a sweater, a battered bag, a belt. Just get some stripes or spots in your life.

Jackie was tough, she was powerful and she was in charge. And so will you be. Nobody tells you to get to the back of the queue if you're in a full-length faux zebra coat. Nobody tells you that yeah, your kid was probably getting on their kid's nerves if you're in leopard-print leggings. Try telling your boyfriend that if he wants to go out with his mates again you might just find someone else. It'll be easier in animal. When your boss calls on Sunday and you're pouring the gravy wearing a cheetah-print sweatshirt he will hear a new strength in your voice and will back down. 'Sorry, stupid idea!' he'll say.

If it's always you getting the coffees in, the vodkas in, organising the trips. If it's you who worries about the atmosphere in the room because you just want everything to be OK and settled and you think this is your job, then it's time to ditch the pleasant cardigans, the 'safe choice' jeans, the completely unremarkable garb.

Anyone who tells you that your look and your clothes are deeply unimportant, just the outside, just salad dressing, is wrong (and usually male). Sometimes we need an armour, a battle outfit. So stop worrying about everyone else (just for a minute) and dress for war. My look for combat (OK, I'm going a little far here) happens to be black clothes, a ton of eye make-up and a fringe. So find yours.

And remember Jackie Collins – author of 32 novels, self-made multimillionaire and one of the sweetest women I've ever interviewed. She was friendly, kind and welcoming but you wouldn't mess with her. That's what you're aiming for, and if a leopard-print clutch is what you need to remind you of this then off you go and find one. Don't let me hold you up.

Quite

OPINIONATED
(I KNOW)

SHOPPING

In our wonderful, confusing, complicated and fascinating twenty-first-century world, there currently exist two ways to shop. The first is in person and the second is online. Living in the Western capitalist society that we do, our economy heavily reliant on consumer goods, you might assume that exchanging our hard-earned money for the myriad items available for sale would be easy, seamless even. We have the cash (plastic) and companies have things that we would like and we just have to do a swap. We even have the internet to help now. But of course in practice, both of these ways to shop are full of challenges.

———

It's a weekday so it's not too busy and we are clacking around Zara/Selfridges/Topshop/H&M and we feel like we're nineteen again. The kids are in school and we're not working. I'm with a friend and we're giddy – this is freedom, this is exciting. Being out, touching fabric, chatting together. I've pulled out shirts, jackets, a sweater.

'After this shall we go for sushi and then will you come with me to buy my mum some soap?'

'Yes, of course. Itsu is an excellent idea. Look at all these shiny clothes. Let's try on everything. This is stupendous. This is like we're in the films, bagsy being Julia Roberts, you can be Cher.'

In our supermarket sweep of picking stuff up there's the occasional 'Can I get away with this? A neoprene bodycon dress in orange?'

'Why the hell not. Of course you can. You're fantastic. You *must* try it on.'

The options are endless, our life is stretched out before us and we're loving it. We're skipping about, oohing and aahing over everything. Our arms are heaving with sweaters and shirts and boyfriend jeans (I have never tried these. This is exhilarating) and everyone is super-friendly – 'Can I get you a different size' and 'That's a great top, it's been very popular this season.'

The woman in the changing room is smiley and upbeat. We count the items. Seven please. I am trying seven things on. Check me out. I might even get more than one – it will feel like I have a whole new wardrobe. Why don't we do this more often? This is life enhancing.

'Can I just give you this enormous black shiny stick to take into the changing room with you?'

'Yes, of course! That would be fantastic,' we say.

We part in the tiny corridor and squeeze ourselves, our bag, our plethora of clothes and the long stick thing into the tiny changing room and, still excited, start trying on. And then, out of nowhere, a massive elephant turd lands on our heads (figuratively speaking).

I wanted a great sweater; it looked really good out there on the hanger with the loud music and my friend cheering me on but now, in this mirror, it looks disgusting. Wait, scrap that – *I* look disgusting. Why am I so tired? Why am I so old? Why am I so wobbly? How come my legs are so short? What happened to my knees? Christ. I try to keep my spirits up and quietly place the offending object back on the hanger but now I'm standing there in mismatched underwear under the ridiculously unforgiving overhead lights. I try on the next thing.

A clingy, one shoulder velvet top? What was I thinking? I'm too old for this. I'm too fat for this. I'm too tired for this.

I can't find the t-shirt I came in wearing, everything is falling off hangers. I am a deflated balloon.

The changing room lady is outside. 'Is everything all right? Let me know if I can get it for you in a different size.' I don't need a different size, I need a different body, I need a darker mirror, I almost certainly need a different face. Help, I don't want these clothes.

My friend and I meet solemnly outside the changing rooms and look directly into each other's eyes but don't say a thing. It's like an unwritten code. We've just seen something bad. Let's not talk about it. Let's just eat some avocado rice tubes dipped in soy sauce and grab some citrus bubble bath and pretend it never happened.

'Any good?' she asks us.

'Uh, no. But thank you so much. Here are the seven items and the stick.'

Retailers – a word please. The second, and I do mean the second, you sort out beautiful soft (really soft, if that's OK) lighting in your changing rooms, the minute you make them slightly bigger than a phone box we'll buy everything.

––––––

That's one way of doing it. The other is shopping online. This, and I do believe I'm not exaggerating, is extremely dangerous. You've had a long day and you're flopping about at home and you enter the world of possibility. An online fashion store. These siren-like pages essentially promise you a different life, a passport to something else. They will gently and seductively whisper that you should buy something for an existence that hasn't materialised yet … but it just might. And you will need something to wear if it does.

Hold on just a second, is that a wicker clutch? A whole bag entirely made up of fancy straw? It's just so magnificent. I want to stroke it, it's crispy, somehow erotic.

Wait, here's a floor-length animal-print kaftan. Wow, I need it, I'll feel like Beyoncé. That will be terribly useful. We might go away, I might be holding a cocktail, I might be wafting around a villa. Yes, let's add that to basket, no question.

Ah, now we're talking, a lemon mohair roll neck and it does look spectacular. That's fantastic, would be great at a lunch in February. And there's a code which means 20 per cent off. I just need to type WINTER20 when they take payment. Brilliant.

While I'm here I might just look at some stuff for the house. Is that a side table in the shape of a bear? I'll just pour myself a glass of wine and come back to it. Hiccup. Gosh, we must have it. I'll even name him. The good news is I can select fast shipping and it will be here for the weekend.

Uh. Stop. Right. There. The problem is that when we're online we shop for a life we don't lead. And there is no moment of deflation, of reckoning, in the lit-like-a-prison changing room to bring us back down to earth. Which, however saddening, at least prevents this shit actually getting into our houses. (Or near our houses – 'Sorry we missed you – please collect from the following depot.')

In the cold light of day I know I will never need a bag that will give me splinters, a scratchy yellow sweater (however good it looks on the model, who is 5'10 and nineteen) or a kaftan, as I will never be on a yacht with Paris Hilton. These aren't me. I won't stop though – I will add and then they come and then I have to return them.

From the comfort of our bedrooms at 11pm during our second glass of wine, we imagine we're going to be climbing up Kilimanjaro (that enormous camo rucksack is excellent, plus it's in a flash sale), we seem to think we're going to be invited to the Oscars (it's floor-length and made of crystals and the plunge front might be a bit much but I could always sew it) and we assume we're going to want to live in a house where woodland creatures are tables/lamps/bedspreads (I realise this is specific, I'm just talking about me here) and we click on the box that says we agree to the terms and conditions and four days later we stand dumbfounded and sheepish when the nice delivery man hands over a hat stand in the shape of a giraffe (yes, me).

———

Shopping is great, it should be empowering, easy, it should make us feel good. But I think we need to approach it realistically and pragmatically. If you are intending to be out, in a store, I'd recommend some make-up and maybe clean hair and possibly dark glasses for the changing room mirror moment. I know it's annoying to go to any trouble but it might make the whole fitting room experience less gruesome.

When shopping at home please don't do it very late (I ordered eight XL packets of Blu Tack at midnight once, just to feel more organised after an especially manic day. We'll never use them all. Ever). And don't drink and click. That's when the owl cushions arrive or the elephant trunk umbrella stand appears (yes, I'm still embarrassed). Sticking to these rules doesn't necessarily help us buy what we do want of course – that perfect pea coat may remain at large for another winter – but it does make for a saner experience and fewer trips to the post office to send it all back. Deep breath and good luck.

AVOID

We've established that friends are important. I hope you have lots of wonderful people in your life – people who you love more than anything, who have your back while you have theirs. If you're sociable and love meeting new people maybe there's still plenty of space in your heart, at your kitchen table, in your WhatsApp groups for more members of the gang. Or perhaps you feel like you barely have enough time to spend with the friends you already have. Quite understandable, but don't shut the doors too firmly. You never know when you might meet someone so brilliant they will be worth making space for. In the main, I love meeting new people – I do think people are generally interesting and wonderful, but equally, there are some people that I think it's often best to avoid …

PEOPLE WHO SHOW YOU PHOTOS ON THEIR PHONE

Oh there he is! Goodness, he can roll over? I understand you're in love with your new puppy. Oh, there's Florence in her school play. Gosh, you've got a new sofa. Wow, I haven't even taken my coat off and your phone is in my face.

Please put it away immediately. If you can't use words then I'm not interested. I've looked at a screen since 9am, we all have. A human, in the flesh. Enough with the showing photos thing.

PEOPLE WHO NAME THEIR CARS

'Come on, I'll take us to the cinema. Just get into Patricia and we'll be off.' Uh, is it OK if we walk?

COUPLES WHO CALL EACH OTHER MUMMY AND DADDY

It's a grown-up dinner, somebody has cooked salmon. We love being with the kids but here we can debate politics, we can swear like troopers, we can shout and laugh and not worry if little Sam has had enough broccoli. Nobody beneath the age of eighteen is present. Yet you hear from a grown woman, 'Daddy, can you grab the ice cream out of the freezer?'

Bye, cheerio. Thanks for having us. Yes, next time at ours! We're just in the middle of a refurb at the moment, though/ we're moving to Copenhagen for a bit/we have a collection of pythons at home that we allow to roam freely so we don't often have people round. I'm changing my number, I'll text you when I get the new one and we'll absolutely find a date.

ANYONE WHO FLIRTS WITH YOUR PARTNER

'Gosh, aren't you a lucky girl?' she says, sighing and not quite meeting your eye. She squeezes his arm. 'He's so manly, so meaty, so delicious!' Her eyes widen in mock shock.

'Do you mind if we swap seats?' she asks. There's that arm squeeze again.

'Let's have lunch! No, let's make it *a deux.*' Air kisses. 'It's your birthday soon isn't it? Promise we'll talk all about you and what he's thinking of getting you.' Is there anything creepier? I'm not possessive, please chat to him, please make him your friend. But the flirting is off-putting.

SHOW-OFFS

'I can't believe it, either. Just the appraisal went so well!'

'No, thing is I've never suffered from hangovers.'

'I am not *trying* to get slimmer, something just seems to be happening. I thought the menopause was supposed to slow down my metabolism? What can I tell you? I've always been different!'

'Yes, we added an extra £100k to the house with the extension, so lucky we did it at the right time!'

'These outfits I put together, they just come naturally to me. Honestly, I don't think it's a big deal, you can call it a skill if you want.'

'Yes, people *have* said I look like Keira Knightley. I think it must be my genes.'

Hurl.

PEOPLE WHO ARE ALWAYS LATE

Look, I've managed to get here on time and my eyes are so bad I can barely read a watch and I too am relying on public transport. I don't want you or anyone to wait for me. But it's OK if I wait for you?

If you want to tell the world you think you're ever so slightly better than them without saying exactly that, always be late. The end.

PEOPLE WHO POP ROUND WITH NO WARNING

'Coo-eee, only us! We've:

> … made a crumble …

> … brought some wine …

> … thought we'd see your new bathroom and check that shower pressure!'

Listen, I want you to come round.

I really, really like you.

But I was about to have a nap. Don't mess with my nap schedule.

PEOPLE YOU FEEL A BIT MEAN AFTER TALKING TO

I like a gossip too. But it can't be mean, not horrible. I don't want to talk at length about people we all spend time with if they're not part of the conversation. There are some friends who want to pick over a friend's relationship, their kids, why they've moved to the new house, why they chose that holiday spot. It's a bit like a double chocolate salted caramel éclair with a honeycomb topping – all fine when you're eating it (ish) and then afterwards you feel a bit yuck, a bit gross.

Avoid the friend who wants you to talk about other friends endlessly. They might imply that it's 'harmless' or frame it as 'I'm a bit worried about them. Why have they got too thin/ fat/loud?' But it's done with faux compassion and it is, let's be honest, unnerving. Plus if he or she does that about other people they supposedly like, what are they saying about you?

PEOPLE WHO ONLY COMPLAIN

He's annoying, the kids are slow, the hairdryer isn't as good as I thought it was going to be. He booked me a massage for my birthday but it was terrible, more of a tickle. We can't find the right holiday villa. Sainsbury's are just delivering too many substitutions these days. I can't find the right tutor for the kids, plus I don't like their schools. My hairdresser talks too much. My local butcher always delivers late. That book everyone said was great wasn't.

I'm going to stop you there. You're lucky. That doesn't mean life has to be only rainbows and unicorns, you don't need to smile the whole time, but you need some perspective. Please get some, then call me.

PEOPLE WHO IGNORE YOU IF THERE'S SOMEONE MORE SUCCESSFUL IN THE ROOM

'Hey, how are you? You look great, where's that top from? What are your plans for the summer?' They're doing all of this but they're not looking at you, they're looking just over your shoulder. You can answer anything – absolutely shit, my neck is covered in semen thank you for asking, we were thinking of going to Hull. They'll nod and smile and reply with 'Wow, great, how smashing, I love it there' because they are not listening and they're basically waiting for someone more interesting/famous/cool to turn up. These people are tools – give them no oxygen.

PEOPLE WHO SAY 'FUNNY' AND DON'T LAUGH

Exactly.

PEOPLE WHO THINK POPULAR CULTURE IS BENEATH THEM

What do I do in my spare time? Listen to Bach mainly. We don't have a television you see. No, the kids don't have phones – they're currently reading Tolkien together at night. We have never tried ice cream from a tub – we just love making our own. What's it like? The fake stuff?

Guys, get a takeaway, watch Ant and Dec, eat a Cornetto in bed. You might be less 'wholesome' but you'll definitely be more fun to be around.

PEOPLE WHO HAVE CONVERSATIONS ON THEIR PHONE WHEN THEY'RE WITH YOU

I have decided not to nap/cuddle my kids/have sex with my husband/shop for calligraphy felt tips online (is this just me?) to be here with you. I have very little interest in hearing your conversation with someone else. I get it, you want to talk to them. Please do it when I've gone. If you're wondering why we don't have lunch anymore then this is it …

PEOPLE WHO THINK THEY'RE THE FIRST TO …

'Guys, guys, you think *you've* been through childbirth but wait till you hear what happened to me.'

'Hey, everyone, you think you've had sex but actually, I've got to say, I've had *major* sex.'

You're not the first, I'm not the first. Stop 'owning' this stuff.

PEOPLE WHO DON'T APPROVE OF SWEARING

Live a little (and stop being a cunt).

PEOPLE WHO WANT TO GET THE DETAILS RIGHT

So the weirdest thing happened last Friday. Hold on, was it Thursday? Now let me see … Usually we get the shopping on a Friday for the weekend but I seem to remember I'd just made a fruit smoothie. Wait, so it's very possible this happened on a Saturday. Hmm, I'll check with Nigel. Ah, he's in the middle of talking. He'll know. Babe. Babe. Nigel, was it on Friday when the thing happened or was it Saturday? I think it might have been Friday. Were you going to golf? Yes, that's it. Agreed. Well, if you had your bacon then it must have been the Saturday. Good. So, Claud. Uh, Claud? Why are those big long pins in your eyes?

NAME-DROPPERS

I don't care who you're friendly with. I'm not interested in who came to dinner. And I really do mean this – nobody (and I do mean nobody) will impress me because I'm solely interested in you. It could be Gloria Hunniford, it could be the Queen, it could be Stevie Wonder. Stop name-dropping them this minute. It doesn't make you cool or popular or awesome, it's a little bit sad.

PEOPLE WHO SAY THEY CARE WHEN THEY DON'T

This is a cause so close to my heart. I really want to help in any way that I can. Yes, it's a wonderful charity. It's name? Um, that escapes me.

PEOPLE WHO SAY THEY DON'T CARE BUT DO

'I'm easy.' 'Always cancel on me, I won't notice.' 'I don't mind where he goes.'

All said while seething, secretly fuming. This is exhausting. Be honest. Better.

SKIING

In the spirit of honesty, I think it's totally safe to say I don't really 'get' any physical activity. I don't believe in yoga (it's the combined odour of feet, avocado and smug that bothers me); group step classes are a form of competitive torture and I've got a tight 10 on how I feel about Pilates. Lift up the pelvic floor with a slight tilt in slow motion in a room that resembles a scene from *Cocoon*. And always in a dank basement surrounded by quiet, serious people in loungewear (can you imagine what I think about loungewear), very slowly rotating their hips on a massive beach ball? 'Keep going! You'll see the results in, say, twelve to eighteen weeks. That'll be 50 quid please.' Come again?

As for the 'I pay someone to come to my house three times a week just to make sure I go for a walk. My personal trainer is now one of my great friends' – I mean, don't even get me started. He comes over, you both chat, he says do a sit-up, he leaves. I had one once, she was lovely and introduced me to lunges. All I can say is it didn't last. Have you ever done a lunge? Well, don't.

I've also never really understood the whole 'we meet in the park at 7am on a Sunday and we wear camo stuff, sometimes a bit of face paint and this really furious man shouts at us and we have to run really fast and shout YES SIR and last week I did so many burpees I was actually sick on myself'. I mean, for *what*? So we can get into the smaller-sized jeans? So our upper arms don't wobble? I've got an idea: get bigger jeans, wear long sleeved t-shirts.

Surely if we just stay in bed, read a book and eat an apple we'll be happier? And, let's be frank, nothing makes anyone quite as ravenous as exercise. I used to swim sometimes and always inhaled two Snickers before I'd even showered. It was a lose-lose situation. And then there was the walking around for the rest of the day with dank hair and a damp towel … The only thing that will make me occasionally opt for the superfood salad over a bucket of pasta is if I've expended absolutely no energy at all. Zing. Bring on the duvet day.

So I think I've made myself clear about exercise in general. But of all the outdoor pursuits, I think I find skiing the most reprehensible. It's not just a sport, a way to get fit, but also seemingly a way of life, a way to holiday, a way to half-term, a way to eat hot cheese (I'll tell you what, save yourself the trouble and come to mine; I'll stick some Cathedral City in the microwave and you can dunk some toast in it). People spend a fortune to fly to a cold mountain (not a holiday) to be surrounded by people shouting, 'Has anyone seen Euripides? I've got his Ralph Lauren gloves.'

It means going somewhere freezing ('but the skies are blue' is simply not enough), waking up early in the morning, grappling with the heaviest, most cumbersome kit known to man (getting on a ski lift whilst wearing skis and holding hats, gloves, sun cream, poles, and a ski pass is horrific) and then hurling yourself down a mountain. People are breaking their limbs all over the place (I'm guessing here) while chucking themselves down steep gradients standing on some sticks. Am I missing something?

Plus, people do all of this whilst also looking glamorous – they're in matching poofy jackets (because it's for the Alps that'll be 400 quid please) and are covered in oversized wraparound glasses and lip gloss. Their children are dropped off with total strangers and then everyone gets blasted at lunchtime.

'Yes darling, it's wonderful. We drop Lucifer and Fru-Fru off with people we've never met before! It's just a rite of passage. The little people really ski well! They can cry a bit when you leave them but then they're off. The key is to start them young, maybe as little as three! They fly down the mountain with wonderful instructors, sure they're hungover, must have been the Jaeger bombs, but it all seems to work. Then we meet them at the restaurant. It's all foie gras and brioche there. You have to try the tuna tartare (note, it's a mountain there are no sodding tuna within a thousand miles of here) – it's extraordinary. And booze of course darling, it's skiing!'

Then there's 'après-ski'. Not being funny but isn't that mainly lolling about? Shouldn't we just call it Sunday? There's a hell of a lot more drinking, some squealing about rosti (look, I like potatoes but I'm not positive they should ever be grated) and lots of chat about black runs and blue runs and well, yawn. There's talk of hot tubs and eating rabbit casserole then everyone has to sober up and dry out their Michelin Man dungarees and it happens all over again the next day.

So skiing. Don't understand it. Can't understand it. Don't want to. Some say it's the best holiday around but I'm not sure those people have been to the Lake District or New York or anywhere in Italy or even their own beds.

If you want to wear some padded clothes and injure yourself while shitfaced, just go to your nearest shopping centre via the off licence. Down a couple of cans, sellotape a duvet around your body and fly down an escalator. Cheaper. And very possibly more fun.

TO BE
HONEST

Los Angeles, oysters, Rubens, pina coladas and getting caught in the rain. All highly overrated. But not quite as overrated as honesty.

'Seriously babe, hand on heart I think I prefer the other dress.' Pardon?

'If you're really asking my opinion then I like it when you make chicken the other way.' Right then. Noted.

'To be honest, I think I liked your hair longer.' To be honest?

To be *honest*? TO BE HONEST?! I'll tell you what, I've got an idea: stop being honest. It seems you do not understand the question 'Does this look OK?' I'm not asking you to actually inspect it. I'm not genuinely checking whether you prefer me in navy or dark grey. I mean, I love you, but you think it's OK to wear a fleece and trainers with jeans. I'm perfectly aware I'm not living with Anna Wintour.

The answer to 'Does this look OK?' is 'Great, baby.' You don't have to give a long answer, you don't have to investigate whether a floor-length or midi skirt is better for my swollen ankles. I'm not really trying to get inside your mind when I ask you if I look half decent. I need you to check whether I have spinach in my teeth or flour on my shirt. 'Do I look OK?' is just

that. Don't look up from your newspaper for more than a second, don't give it any thought. A 'lovely' or 'fine' will do.

And then there's: 'I'm sure you've thought about it, but to be
truthful …' If the first bit of that sentence is genuinely true
then you don't need to continue. You think I should breastfeed
for longer, eh? If it was you, you'd let them suckle till they're
two? That's great, that's fine. If your three-year-old was trying to get into your bra in the coffee shop I can promise you I
wouldn't lean forward and say, 'Truthfully, I think you should
give her a sippy cup.' I just wouldn't.

'Sincerely, I think you should consider not doing that job any
more.' What? Why? Why are you saying 'sincerely', because
I don't really think it's sincere. Look mate, I've got a mortgage
to pay and eyeliner to buy.

And these professions of honesty are so often followed by
disclaimers, appeals for tolerance of a completely unasked-for
opinion. 'Please don't take this the wrong way…' You know that
I might, otherwise it wouldn't have occurred to you to say it. So
why not just nod and say you like it, are happy for me, and move
on? The worst of these is 'No offence, but …' That, surely, is
just announcing that you are going to say something offensive.

Opinions can hurt, they can cause upset and I'm not convinced they're entirely necessary. You're at your mum's and
she's repainted the loo. It's a dusky pink with a bottle green
towel display (she's fashioned the top one into a swan) but she's
really pleased with it. She's literally bursting with pride. This
is what to say: 'It looks excellent, Mum, I love it, well done.'

My friend has just started going out with someone who
seems like a bit of an arse. I don't say, 'He's a muppet, you could
do so much better.' I'm not suggesting we all have to love him
but if she's currently enamoured what's the point in bringing
her down? I go round to someone's house and he's made float-
ing islands for dessert (I don't know about you but I actually
can't think of a worse pudding, it's just way too wet) and, guess
what, I eat it.

Opinions: keep them to yourself unless you're sitting with your best friend and they seriously want to know something. Then, of course, spill.

There's so much importance placed on honesty, or maybe it should be called fake honesty and it's simply not useful. Appraisals, how-are-you-doing-meetings, 360s, people telling you what they *really* think. Here's an idea – why not just swallow it down? The greatest people to be around are positive people. I think you look smashing; I think the job is fine; I bet he didn't mean it when he got a bit twatty with the waiter. What they are really saying here is 'I'm on your side'. Miles better. Encouraging, supportive, kind, less forthright, way less judgemental.

The world is full of people shouting their opinion, who can't wait to tell us all what they think (have you been on Twitter recently? A load of people angrily shouting at the moon, literally throwing a sock into space). What I want and need from my family and friends is simply 'That's a good idea.'

When we really need to share truth and feelings and worries about each other then of course we'll come clean and we'll wipe up the mess afterwards. You seem to be getting drunk a lot more than you used to; she doesn't make you happy; you seem to be screaming at your kids a lot. That's proper stuff – the real deal. Everything else is just noise. Why does everyone think their opinion is the right one anyway?

There is no right. Love him, don't love him; send her to private school, send her to the local comp. Honestly, live your bloody life because it's hard enough. I'm right over here cheerleading you on. Go on, you've absolutely got this. And if it all goes to shit I've got a bottle of tequila, a toasted sandwich maker and all of Oasis on vinyl. It'll be fine.

HELP

Here's an important thing.

Help.

You should, I should, we should always, always, ask for it.

I mean it. We're not good at asking for support and that's got to change. You feel wobbly, overwhelmed, it's all a bit too much, the boiler's buggered, you're not getting stuff right, you get angry over little things and when the oven went on the blink you cried. Get help.

Don't feel like you're doing something wrong, don't think you're being a pain, get rid of the 'but they won't care' that's rolling around your head.

Asking for help is the most natural thing in the world to a child. Can you lift me up? Please can I have a fork. Why does my chemistry teacher say this? Can you give me a hand with my room? Why doesn't the shower switch on, please can you have a look at it? I feel a bit down today, do you know why? They ask and we don't think less of them, we don't think that they're weak, that they can't cope. We answer 'Of course!' or 'Give me a second' and we jump in. And we love, and I really believe this, lending a hand.

In our teens we still ask for it and then all of a sudden we get all self-conscious and nervous and we don't want to be a burden, to show we're vulnerable. Sure, we call our parents and give them all the bad news – I'm knackered, I think we're going to break up, I'm not going to get that promotion, I'm short of money – but to everyone else everything is fine. How are you? Great. How's the family? Fantastic. Everything OK at work? Loving it.

I don't know when we decided we had to be brave, to go it alone, to tackle everything head-on by ourselves. Maybe we feel insecure, we don't want to test our friends, test our bond. We think, 'I'd like to ask them but what if they say no? Then I'll find out they don't care enough, they don't feel the same way I do about them.' I don't know when it got awkward just straight out saying 'I need you', 'I'm not coping' or 'Help me'.

It's possible the worry, the angst, the grit is too complicated to unravel. Sometimes explaining the problem is too much of a problem in itself. It feels easier to say 'Yeah, everything's OK' rather than trying to untangle the knots. But there are still so many different ways we can help others and they can help us.

HELP WITH WORK

If it all feels like it's going a bit too fast or much too slow and you can't seem to see your path, then find a mentor or speak to someone you trust who's got a bit more experience than you. It doesn't have to be in the same industry. Ask an uncle, an aunt, the person at the office who's friendly and just solicit their advice. What should I do now? Any chance they'd consider me for this job?

Nobody minds, nobody thinks, 'God, why is she bothering me?' People like being helpful, they like stepping in, they like knowing their opinion counts for something. Ask. Don't sit there and seethe or feel unhappy as someone else is promoted/picked for the trip abroad/given a different-sized bonus. Find a person and ask for help.

I have relied on people who know more than me (that's a lot of people) throughout my working life. When standing in at Radio 2 recently, I realised I'd mixed one song into another exceedingly badly. A lovely studio manager helped me. He literally solved the problem in under five minutes. I was over-whelmed by the buttons (it's like a space ship) and so I asked for guidance. He wasn't grumpy or put out but just terrifically, indescribably helpful. I was so happy that the next day I got into work extra early just to practise. Thank you, Nick.

HELP WITH DECORATING

Doing up a home is completely overpowering for some; even fixing up a room can feel like an insurmountable challenge (I'm talking about me, see page 181). You can choose make-up, can cook a great poached egg (I'm not talking about me here, still confused about the whole cling film option) but when it comes to paint colour and picking a rug it's all way too much. There's so much choice and too many shops to wander about. I'll just go to John Lewis and pick from there. Why is everything lilac or apricot? I don't want a rug with birds on it. How do people do this? I want to curl up. Help.

Don't do it alone. Don't try and be the master of everything. Go and see a friend whose house you like and ask them to ex-plain. I had to do this. I knew what I wanted it to look like but had no idea how to get there.

My friend is exceptional at houses – she's not particularly interested in coats or shoes but can do a good 40 minutes on what makes a good table and the size of plates you want (not massive ones, anything you put on them looks miserly, plus they are a pain to wash up and store – magical advice). Meet her at a market or take her for tea or show her photos of things you like and ask her to help. It's like a science, something to do with layering, cushions, curtains, blankets, side tables, where to get a bed. I loathe that jazz; she does not and she basically sorted my life out. Do I start with a lone candle or a bath I asked? She took me in hand. Get help.

HELP WITH THE KIDS

I know your mum did it all. She did the weekly shop when having it delivered was not an option – dealing with a screaming baby, supermarket lighting and carrying six bags of tins and toilet paper to the car, or on the bus, on two buses. Not fun by yourself, exhausting with a papoose. She did that plus a full-time job and she turned up to your nativity play, your parent-teacher meeting on time and kept the house tidy and often cooked supper. Yes, a superwoman.

Well, this is now and the office doesn't stop (that small gadget in your back pocket means you're never, ever off) and the schools expect you to do more at home so, guess what? You need some help. If you're with the kid's dad then they must step up. It's not OK if you are doing 90 per cent of it and then he gets a pat on the back if he takes them to a park for a morning. If your partner is working all the time you might need a nanny or a cleaner or an au pair, if you can afford it, or share one of the above with a friend.

Relinquish the boots, make-up, night out and get help in any way that you can. Ask your neighbour or a friend to come round for the afternoon. *It is too much to do by yourself.* You are not failing, you are not less of a mother, you are not letting anyone down. When it gets on top of you – ask for help.

My grandparents picked me up from school every Wednesday so my mum always knew she could work late. My parents tuck my kids up in bed if my husband and I are working. We're lucky as they live near but I'm fully aware this doesn't exist for everyone.

Find someone to take at least something off your plate – even if that's just cleaning the kitchen once a week. Or reciprocal childcare with another family you know who are busy and could also use some time to dash to the shops. I think we all need to be explicitly given permission to say I can't do this by myself and someone needs to step in.

HELP WITH A RELATIONSHIP

You've been together for a while and the union has got scratchy, annoying. You're scrappy with each other. He wants to know where the mustard is and you want to rip his head off. Everything is fine and then, one day, it just isn't. Ask for help.

If you don't want to make the enormous leap to a therapist's sofa then ask someone to watch the kids when you go away for a night. Ask your friends whether it's worthwhile staying with him or if it's better to cut the cord. Don't think it's OK to always feel unhappy/miffed/out of sorts. Just ask for help.

And also, ask him. You have to be able to say, 'You're making me sad/why am I in charge of mustard?/we don't cuddle any more/I think you might be a bit of a dick.' If you don't want to ask an outside party for help with him, then get help from him.

HELP WITH CLOTHES

I am not suggesting you get a stylist here. I'm also not saying you should pay someone a fortune to work out what season best suits you (here, I'll do it for free: winter) but definitely book in for some personalised shopping. Loads of the big shops have this service and it's fantastic. Go with a friend – to Topshop, to Selfridges, to any big department store near you and just say, 'I'm bored of wearing the same clothes, I've worn them for twenty years straight. I need some ideas' and before you know it you'll be trying on things you'd never have considered.

There's no obligation to buy, so if you go somewhere fancy just take in all the info and then get what you want elsewhere. The excellent people who work in these departments want to help. I promise. It's their actual job and they're bloody fantastic at it. I once went to a jeans department with two friends and we spent a good three hours (yes, it was before kids) working out if high-waisted or mid-waisted was better (it's always the latter).

Here's the thing with help. People want to do it. We get really stuck sometimes and just need to unload, to spill the dirt, to share the burden. Think about you. Do you get grumpy if someone asks for advice, if someone sends you their justgiving. com link, if a friend calls to have a little cry? Do you mind? Of course you don't. You race round, you donate, you offer your services. Help. The more you give the more you get.

THEY'RE GOING TO LEAVE, AREN'T THEY?

So your small person is big, properly big, maybe six feet tall. They're talking about leaving home during Sunday lunch (this makes you cry a bit but you hide it under your fringe while you're handing out potatoes) and they are full of chat about fresher's week and bars, dating and beers. They ask if they're allowed to take posters and if their for-teenagers credit card will work. (Sure, I like seeing what they buy – I especially like it when I catch him out. 'Mum, I went to Rymans.' That's weird because they must be selling highlighter pens in Chicken Cottage.) They mention bean bags and laundry baskets and which detergent they should use. It all feels like they're doing it to taunt you because you simply can't deal with the idea of them leaving home. They're not, they're just seriously excited about their upcoming adventure, but this is how it feels.

Of course, when they were little you dreamed of them getting into a great university – you sat next to them helping them (ish) with maths, imagining visiting them at Oxford or Leeds. They were eight then and had just learnt how to divide numbers and you'd stroke their hair and kiss their noses and get them little snacks (all homework is easier with Mini Cheddars, this is a proven fact) and you'd wonder if they would prefer Edinburgh or Manchester.

I bet he/she will like studying classics or maybe they'll be a bio scientist. I'll go and visit like my parents did when I was eighteen and we'll buy them steak and things they can never afford. We'll go up on the train carrying plants they won't water and tidy their room and meet their new friends. This is what it's all about – getting an education so they can be fully fledged grown-ups and their brains can expand, even flourish. What a privilege, what a chance, how fantastic, we thought.

But you see, it was so far away. It was safe to fantasise about graduations and his first boy- or girlfriend and visiting for cream teas and us fake moaning about taking down clean pants and now he's big and he's going and I'm going to be frank, I can't bear it.

What do you mean, you'll just be back for only some of the holidays? Can you explain again why you wouldn't just prefer to get a job? You wouldn't build up so much debt, you could live here (no, I promise you will no longer have a curfew) or why don't you study in London? There's a college just round the corner. Yes, just go there. The child (sorry, almost man) mentions something about wanting to be somewhere far away. He says he wants independence (cruel) and wants some space (there's space here. You have your own room, you don't share anymore, we fixed the shower – what else do you want?). Regarding space, university digs are tiny. I'm just saying …

I'm no longer interested in him expanding his brain. He seems bright enough. He reads books when I bug him and he has a pretty solid knowledge of socialism and conservatism and knows about the environment. He can keep up in a conversation about Mandela or Shakespeare, he has a solid knowledge of the boxsets on Netflix. What else exactly does he need to know that he can't discover through discussion and reading?

We all know that what we really learnt at university was how to drink and how to have sex. I'm happy for him to learn both those things while he lives with us, here. He works at Five Guys every holiday and it's his favourite job, he wants to work in a bar or restaurant, he's dazzled by the hospitality industry. Why does he need to fill his head with politics and history in order to do well? Why can't he just stay with me? I know this is selfish and I know he'll have to leave but I don't know how I'll cope. All his life he's been just right here – at every breakfast, at the weekends, after school, sitting next to me when we watch movies. He's a good chatter and an excellent sibling. He's funny, he's kind and he's (this is bad, isn't it?) *ours*.

But I know the time has come to share him. For him to have a bedroom somewhere else. It's time for him to work out how to make garlic bread (it's his favourite) and I suppose it's time for him to make mistakes. To lose the credit card, to break his phone, to get into trouble with mates for disappearing/drinking too much/flirting with the girl one of them fancies. It's time for him to deal with bills and shopping and handing in work on time without me reminding him. It's definitely time for him to live his life. But here's the thing – when I look at him he's still four.

He's still hurtling down a slide or eating a miniature yoghurt or giggling in the bath. He's still ambling into our bed if he had a bad dream and he's still trying to cook garlic bread by putting it in the toaster (I can't even) and he's still small. He's the reason we jump out of bed to ask how he slept, he's the reason we stay up till midnight on a Saturday so that we know he's back safe from the party. He's the reason we go to burger places if we eat out and he's the reason I buy Haribo.

He's also the real reason my life is as great as it is. I know that's too much pressure, too much to put on a soul. I know he won't read this (genuinely) but I can positively say that everything was grey before I had him. I know for many people kids aren't the answer, and I know I don't love him more than other people love their children. That's not what I'm saying. I'm just saying he's *my* answer. I don't know what I was doing before having children but it was very meh, all a bit nothing. He and his brother and sister gave me an anchor, a life, a family and now he's breaking away. Of course I'll let him leave and I know he'll rent a flat with mates and then meet someone and that's how it has to be. If we do our job properly, we equip them with everything they need and then we let them go. My brain tells me this is right, even my gut. But my heart isn't having it.

What a time he'll have. We'll pack his bags and roll up the posters and remind him at least 100 times to call home (which he won't) but it will hurt. If you're reading this and are younger than me, if you think I've lost my mind then I get it. I was like you too. There is no moral to this story, there's no pithy end line for the close.

Jake, if you ever do read this then please know it's been the greatest privilege of my life to live with you for eighteen years. Please call me occasionally and know that this is your home, it always will be. Please don't lose your credit card, be great to your friends and even greater to your partner. I love you.

AND FINALLY...

I realise that a lot of people are keen to give you advice. Whether you have asked for it or not (I'm specifically talking about me here and yes, I'm sorry for being bossy about the whole wearing black thing) but now we've reached the end (seriously, thank you so much for reading this) I'd like to share some advice that doesn't come from me, but that has been passed down to me and has made a real difference. I try to follow all of this but of course, sometimes I've failed ...

DO YOUR HOMEWORK

There are many phrases I remember from my childhood – 'Go back to bed', 'They're smaller than you so be nice', 'Turn that Duran Duran down'. But the main one is: 'Do your homework'.

Always, always 'Do your homework.' Put in the time, use a highlighter if you need one (nothing takes me back to my finals more than a yellow Stabilo Boss) and get it done. Make notes, write an essay plan, work out what you're going to say, find out what the teacher wants. 'Go back upstairs Claud, and whatever you do, do your homework.' It was a recurring joke. OK, Mum, we get it. Do it properly, read the question more than once, make it neat, basically – concentrate.

It stayed with me. If I am interviewing someone then I read everything they've ever said. If I am going to a work dinner I look up the people who are going to be there. Sometimes I've failed, I've decided to wing it and it's always showed – I've flopped. When I haven't read the book I've faltered, talked a lot about the font, mentioned the dedication and wavered. People can always tell.

We all try and make everything look effortless, we downplay what we've done – what, this old dress? I just scrabbled together what was left in the fridge. Yeah, liked the look of Cambridge so I applied, I fancied being a TV presenter so gave it a go and it just happened. But that's not always the whole truth. Sometimes we need to pull our fingers out, sometimes it's going to be hard going, sometimes it might even be a slog.

If I can pass on one thing, let it be this: you think you know enough? Go back and check, do your homework. Yes, I've tried to instil this in the kids and yes, they hate me.

BE A GEEK

People will say wearing glasses is undesirable. Having your hair tied up and being stuck in a book is distant, not very sociable. What's wrong with her? She wants to be an engineer? Good god. Why doesn't she put a nice dress on and get some contact lenses and come and chat with us? Why doesn't she want a beer? She's seventeen! What's so interesting about chemistry anyway? You'd think she'd want to make the most of herself, get out there, meet some boys. She's such a do-gooder, a real bookworm, shame. You must feel a bit disappointed.

I cannot say this strongly enough. Girls, listen to me when I tell you to nerd the fuck up. Do not be tempted by the 'fun' (you can have fun at Harvard or Oxford, or when you're running

Apple) but be a full-time weed, be bookish, be stand-offish and get lost in maths, in science, in literature. There's nothing, absolutely nothing, wrong with being a geek. The nerdier the better. You don't need glasses? Get some anyway. And braces too while we're at it. The boys I met at sixteen thought I was a dork, a bore and not hip enough to be with them, they'd make fun of us for staying in and having hairy upper lips, thick frames and sensible rucksacks (yes, we religiously used both straps). That's OK. They were, in many respects, bang on but me and my girls did alright in the end.

MANNERS MATTER

I'm not talking about dabbing your mouth with a napkin. I'm talking about saying please and thank you and writing notes. Sounds simple, sounds easy. Because I'm old you can take it from me, nobody forgets a thank-you text, a 'It was lovely to see you, hope the meeting/date/weekend with the future in-laws goes OK.' Everyone remembers a great message of support.

If you're doing work experience along with a bunch of other young people and you're the most polite it will get noticed. It sounds extremely old fashioned and can be time consuming but manners just are important. Thanks for explaining, please can I ask a question, a follow up note. Yes, yes I sound like your mother.

DON'T COMPARE AND CONTRAST

Evaluate sweaters, weigh up the differences between your local restaurants, check all the holidays on offer before you purchase. That's good common sense.

But don't compare yourself to humans. It's a mantra I was taught early and am so grateful for it. They've got a better kitchen, her boss clearly admires her more as she's getting a company car, they must be more in love because they held hands all night. They have a fully trained dog, why does ours jump up, eat all our socks and mount Grandma? It always leads to misery, it's unfair (both on them and you) and, without being too dramatic, it ends today.

Of course they have a better kitchen, it's made out of solid marble, FFS. Don't stress. They'll be prettier, cleverer too, and funnier (this one hurts the most) and they will be more in love. Be happy for them, life might not always go their way, something might be round the corner, so please don't begrudge them the immaculately behaved miniature schnauzer, the great sex, the respect from their boss or the happiness. When they feel joy, feel it with them.

It's just not sustainable to constantly worry about what everyone else is doing and if they've got it better. And if they do – maybe it's genes, it's luck, or perhaps it's because they might just be … better. And that's more than OK. You want to be good enough for your parents and your siblings and your partner and your friends and, if you have them, your kids. Everything else is just croutons. Don't want somebody's life, take full responsibility for your own.

Also, while we're here maybe let's spend a second on people who post their flawless life. Our real friends reveal all the good and the bad but there are others whose life looks just like a postcard, like a movie.

They're doing a star jump on a beach, their kids are in matching seersucker cotton shirts with perfect scruffy hair and beaming smiles, their house looks just right. Their lunch is perfectly placed and looks both delicious and healthy (I have yet to believe this food exists but I remain optimistic).

Maybe their life isn't necessarily better than yours, maybe they just choose to show you the best bits and filter out the rest. Why are they not just serving up fluffy pancakes topped with some homemade organic compote? That would be the thing to do, I reckon. Gather the kids and family together for movie night with personalised tartan blankets but then maybe just, you know, live it instead of posting it.

Know that if someone is constantly looking for validation, if they're saying 'Look at us, isn't it great?' well, it might not be great. I love social media but it took me a while to grasp this. Know that every great photo has been maybe taken three or four times. It's not an accident she/he looks slim/is laughing/is holding the perfect glass of wine against the perfect backdrop. It's not perfect as if it was perfect they wouldn't have to stop to take a photo. Why isn't living it simply enough, why would they want to show every minute, every avocado on toast, every view from their hotel window? I'm not saying they're evil or are intentionally trying to make their friends jealous (that's preposterous, we're talking about grown-ups here) but it's almost like if they haven't captured it and shown it, maybe it didn't happen?

Please remember a post is often, well, a boast. Your life is just as great. You managed to be at the zoo at the right time and saw the penguins being fed; he brought you a cup of coffee and ruffled your hair; she got a good mark in her biology even though she's yet to fully grasp photosynthesis. Comparing and contrasting is excellent and useful for bars and coats and cat breeds – not cool for people. Wish them well (I hope he gets a raise, she should buy and wear that coat, am so happy their kids tan easily and play trombone) and be delighted for them.

MAKE THE TEA

I don't care where you are in the company hierarchy, I don't care if you're Mark Zuckerberg. If you're with people and hot drinks are going to be drunk, bloody make them. This is (apart from the others) my favourite bit of advice from my dad.

Don't be uppity, don't think, 'Woo hoo now I have a PA, I won't have to deal with the kettle!' That's ridiculous and pompous and your office will hate you (they will not say this to your face). Make a cup of tea for your PA too. 'Hello Tom, hope you had a good weekend, I'm getting the coffees in, can I get you one?'

I'm not allowed to talk about people who have taken part in *Strictly* (I think) but I'd like to mention Ed Balls here. We always all meet for the first time on a day in August, that's how it works – all the dancers and the celebrities taking part. We didn't know anything about Ed at this point. We saw this man at the coffee station. 'Can I interest anyone in a custard cream? Daisy, did you say two sugars?' and we loved him from that day forward. He wasn't doing it for show, he wasn't, 'Yes, I was the shadow chancellor, look at me being all normal.' He just simply wanted to get everyone a warm drink. This continued throughout the series. Want a cup of tea? Ask Ed.

SAY AN EARLY NO

Hey, do you want to come to ours for a kitchen supper next month? (I can't tell you how much I hate this phrase. Do other rooms have meals? Do people have bathroom brunches, hallway snacks?) Some new neighbours are coming round that we've just met and we're only a 50-minute drive from you. Although if I'm honest it can be slightly longer if the A40 is bunged up. But we'd love to see you! Alex will make his special lamb surprise.

Wait. Hold on. Let's screech to a halt. Before you reply, 'Great, sounds lovely, 50 minutes is nothing, it'll be a good chance for us to listen to that podcast we keep hearing about,' let's look into the future for a sec. You know now you won't want to go, you know that at the beginning of that week, when you hit the diary app to see what you have planned, your heart will sink.

The day comes and you just can't face it. You're knackered, the house is a mess, you've got an early start tomorrow, you actually don't like lamb and now you will have to make an excuse about work/babysitting problems/the ceiling falling in. So say no. Say no now. Sorry we can't. You're too far away. They won't be angry (please never think you're irreplaceable) and you'll be so happy you don't have to drive for an hour to eat a half lamb tagine/half lamb curry with a group of people you've never met before.

An Early No (capitalised to make my point) should be applauded. My mum taught me this when I was at university and a friend invited me to a computer science student weekend in Cardiff. It was going to be three days of discussing modems (it was definitely going to be more complicated than this but you get the gist). Now, complete nirvana if coding is your thing. I ummed and ahhed and said yes and then said maybe and finally, the night before, a no and actually our friendship never fully recovered. Basically I gave them the run-around and it was extremely annoying. Just because you're asked to do something it doesn't mean you have to say yes. Don't think you're letting them down with a no, know that you're seriously letting them down with a no on the day.

NOTHING HAPPENS AFTER MIDNIGHT

You know those nights when you're teetering between 'Yeah, think it's time to go' and 'OK then, one more drink'? I can tell you now that the first is a better option. Leave. Go. Vamoose. Jump on a bus, on a tube, in a car. You never regret leaving, you only regret staying. My mum always said, 'Nothing that interesting happens after midnight,' and she's right. Definitely go, drink a couple of drinks, eat tacos, have a laugh but then escape and get tucked up. Otherwise it gets messy, you're miles away from home and you'll feel completely rubbish the next day.

If you're under the age of 30 you must obviously ignore this message.

LOVE FIERCELY

Let it take a while when you meet someone. Be casual, be aloof, be busy. Be a bit 'Yeah, I'll check that date,' rather than readily available. Don't be 'Call me any time' and don't always pick up the phone on the second ring. People will tell you this is game playing, that you should just be upfront and in love but I'm not interested in that. Not because I want him to be keener but just to protect yourself. Don't go all in straight away. Be a little mysterious (I'm not suggesting a Hamburglar mask at this point) but have other stuff going on.

However, once you do decide to dive in then do it with passion. Envelop him, love him to bits, make him feel good and be kind. Love him with every bit of you. If he turns out to be a dick then, sorry (it happens), but at least you've given it everything.

As for the kids and the pets, tell them you love them till you're hoarse. Don't save it for special occasions – they'll look bored with it, they'll eye-roll, the teenager will grunt and might refuse to say it back but he'd miss it if it wasn't there. Put the mugs away, I love you. Call me after your test, I love you. Don't take drugs if they're being passed around, I love you. That kind of shizz. Let it be your full stop.

CLAUD, IT'S NOT A COMPETITION

Right. This is the big lesson. The end of the conference wrap-up. This is the closing speech. We've all had a pleasant time (I hope) and now I'm handing out the party bags. So here we go.

It's not a competition. It's not a race. That's it. That's what I was told and that's what I believe.

When we're at school we're applauded if we do well. We work and work and work and we get our grades and we fill out the UCAS form and hope for the best. Magically we do OK and then, again, we try and try and try. We don't need to do spectacularly well (seriously, have you met the people who got firsts?) but we definitely need to pass.

Then there's the race to get a job. Which one should I go for? Will I ever get a mortgage if I do that? Will I be able to go out with my credit card and, you know, pay a bill? Can I keep my head above water? Will I earn enough to move out of home and will I ever meet someone who I want to kiss more than twice?

Argh, I should be ovulating today – we'll do it twice so it clicks and beds into my womb. They have a garden; we need a garden. They're getting a kitten – quick, let's get a prettier one.

It was a late lesson I'll grant you, but this is the real biggie. Don't compete. And here's why. There are no medals. I know. It was a shock to me too. There just aren't. You don't turn 70 and get a knock on the door: 'Hello, I believe you've done rather brilliantly in the whole life stakes. You got those window boxes up before your neighbours, you managed to keep that job for longer than everyone thought, you're still reasonably slim for someone who loves macaroni cheese so much and well done on that breastfeeding! You've won. Do you mind following me as there's a ceremony in Trafalgar Square? It starts at midday. You're just after the man who made wonderful apple pies and before the woman who always walked the dog in the rain.'

Look, do the very best you can. Cuddle those you love, work hard but that marathon you think you're running? It's not there so just come off the track. I'll repeat it (as a friend had to do for me). There. Is. No. Race. That finishing line is invisible, it's just a figment of your imagination, so stop trying to reach it before the others. We're here for five minutes; enjoy the view.

ACKNOWLEDGEMENTS

This book only exists because of two brilliant people. If you loathe it, please blame Holly Bott and Amanda Harris (I'm very happy to give you their contact details). I absolutely wouldn't have considered it without their push, their brains and their endless support. They also gave me a lanyard, which I feel is important to mention.

My enormous thanks to everyone at HQ who were so lovely and charming on Zoom and said this was a good idea. I can't wait to actually physically meet you all. As promised, I'll bring biscuits and we can do the conga. My heartfelt thanks go to my editor Kate Fox. She's the kindest person on the planet and made cinnamon buns, which as we all know are the answer to everything.

Thank you to the extraordinary Jonathan Yeo. I still quite can't believe you drew me for the cover. I will be in shock about this fact for the next hundred years.

Thanks to my extraordinary girlfriends – for the laughs, for your wisdom, for your love. I don't know how I got so lucky to have you all but am grateful every single day. Regarding this book, I need to say an enormous and specific thank you to Sara, Vicky, Imi, Hen and Kirsty.

I need to say thank you to the people who got me here in the first place. On both the telly and happily tapping away on a computer writing gibberish. I will be grateful forever to Joanna Kaye, Jonathan Lloyd, Martin Ivens and Simon Kelner. Thank you to the BBC for a career I don't deserve and thank you to every single person who works on *Strictly*.

Thank you to my knockout parents and step-parents for being the best people I know, and finally to the Danish creature I call husband. Kris, I know I've been annoying writing this – complaining and moaning and never getting dressed and insisting on toast and lemon curd at midnight while you've basically done everything else. Thank you for pretending to be totally fascinated by my use of brackets. (I love you so much.)